Fiction and Emotion

To the memory of
my father

Bhuban Hatiboruah

FICTION AND EMOTION

A Study in Aesthetics and the Philosophy of Mind

BIJOY H. BORUAH

CLARENDON PRESS • OXFORD

1988

Oxford University Press, Walton Street, Oxford OX2 6DP
New York Toronto
Delhi Bombay Calcutta Madras Karachi
Petaling Jaya Singapore Hong Kong Tokyo
Nairobi Dar es Salaam
Melbourne Auckland
and associates in
Berlin Ibadan

Oxford is a trade mark of Oxford University Press

Published in the United States
by Oxford University Press, New York

This edition is not for sale in South Asia

British Library Cataloguing in Publication Data
Data available

Library of Congress Cataloguing in Publication Data
Data available

Phototypeset in Times by Spantech Publishers Pvt Ltd
708 Pragati Tower, 26 Rajendra Place, New Delhi 110008
Printed by Rekha Printers Pvt Ltd, New Delhi 110020

CONTENTS

PREFACE

The origin of this book can be traced back to my vague romantic fascination with the 'fictional' emotions that we experience imaginatively: how, as children, we weep over the fate of Pinocchio and, as adults, feel sadness reading about the plight of Desdemona and terror in the face of the blackbirds in Hitchcock's *The Birds*. With time this fascination developed into a reflective concern, which in turn led to a deromanticization of earlier fascination. Imbibing the philosophical spirit, I began to look for the conditions of the possibility of experiencing fictional or 'imagined' emotions. What I have arrived at is a theory of fictional emotion, or emotional response to fiction, that can account for the rational justification of such responses in view of the role of works of fiction in our understanding of human reality.

Put in systematic terms, this work is at once a study in philosophical aesthetics and in the philosophy of mind. The problem of explaining how we feel towards fictional characters and events, despite our clear knowledge and belief that the putative objects of our response are fictitious, has been the central concern in this work. In dealing with this problem one is necessarily led to examining the relations between emotion and belief, belief and fiction, and fiction and imagination. Indeed, it should be clear to anyone in philosophy that most problems in philosophical aesthetics require taking recourse to studies in the philosophy of mind.

An earlier version of this work was submitted as a doctoral dissertation to the University of Guelph, Guelph, Ontario, Canada. I acknowledge my deepest gratitude to Professor Douglas Odegard, who persevered through several years in supervisory work that was most necessary in completing this book. Other philosophers whom I cannot help remembering for their advice and encouragement are Albert Shalom of McMaster University and Brian Calvert of the University of Guelph. To Professor Roger Scruton of Birkbeck College, University of London, I owe a special debt of gratitude for furnishing me with insightful ideas after having examined my doctoral dissertation.

I am grateful to the editor of the *Journal of the Indian Council of Philosophical Research* for permission to include my paper 'Emotion and Belief' in this book as its first chapter.

Bijoy H. Boruah

INTRODUCTION

Emotions constitute a fertile field for philosophical cultivation. From Aristotle to Sartre philosophers have devoted considerable attention to the analysis of the nature and role of the emotions in human experience and behaviour. In contemporary analytical philosophy various works have been done both on the nature of emotion in general and on the nature of individual emotions such as fear, jealousy, pride and envy—thus placing the emotions in the forefront of problems in the philosophy of mind and moral psychology.

There is, however, a large untracked terrain in the field of emotion that has not been sufficiently explored. This is the terrain of the various emotions that we feel in response to fiction. Fictional characters and events, depicted in works of art, are as much objects of our emotional attitudes as real people and actual situations. But this plain fact is also surprising, since it makes us wonder how we are able to respond to fiction in ways that are in many respects characteristically similar to our response to real life. Thus a contemporary philosopher, Nicholas Wolterstorff, remarks: 'How does one explain the fact that the world of a painting, of a film, of a novel, of a play, moves one profoundly, inducing fear, grief, exhilaration, etc. all the while never stirring one from the conviction that what is represented never happened, and certainly is not happening now'. (Wolterstorff, 1980, p. 366) Although Wolterstorff does not address himself to this problem, he believes that remarkably little attempt has been made to answer the question.

In the present book my aim is to state clearly this problem and provide a satisfactory solution in the light of other major proposals put forward by some contemporary philosophers. I trace the origin of this problem in an article by Colin Radford, who maintains that our emotional responses to fiction—or what I prefer to call fictional emotions—involve us in incoherence and inconsistency. The incoherence is that of belief: we believe that what we see or read about in a work of fiction is unreal or non-existent; yet we respond to a fictional character or event with a certain emotion which can only be explained by imputing to us the very belief that is rationally impossible to form. Fictional emotions are thus held to be rationally inexplicable. There seems to be a paradox about belief underlying these emotions and Radford persistently claims that this paradox is inescapable.

In order to realize the force of this paradox it is necessary at first to understand the nature and role of belief in situations involving emotion. I therefore provide in Chapter One an analysis of the relation between emotion and belief. I argue that appropriate beliefs play both a conceptual and a causal role in the evocation of paradigm human emotions. In so far as an emotion is founded on a suitable belief, this belief constitutes a *reason* for having the emotion and, hence, the belief plays a conceptual role in the constitution of the emotion. But the belief also plays a *causal* role in the occurrence of the emotion. I spell out the nature of this causation by distinguishing between an evaluative belief and an existential belief and by explaining the causal potency of beliefs in terms of a dynamic psychological structure. This psychological structure, formed mainly out of a person's evaluative beliefs, is activated when he is presented with an emotion-evoking object or situation. The disposition to feel and react in a certain way is actualized by his existential belief about the given object or situation.

The problem of fictional emotions arises from the question as to how we can identify the required belief that constitutes the reason for an emotional response to a fictional character or event, and how we can describe the application of the normal causation of real-life emotions in a modified form.

In Chapter Two I give a critical exposition of Radford's charge of the irrationality of our emotional responses to fiction—his view that such a response occurs without satisfying the necessary condition for a mental state's being an emotional response, namely the involvement of a suitable belief. I consider whether he is justified in treating these responses as *emotions* if he denies that they satisfy the necessary condition for being an emotion. My criticism hinges on the argument that any emotional state must be minimally or structurally rational. In this context I also discuss an alternative proposed by Peter Lamarque and Michael Weston and try to show why it is not viable.

Radford's charge of irrationality is counterintuitive in that it conflicts with our normally recognized rationality of aesthetic experience. Besides, many philosophers of art find emotional responses to works of fiction not just unpuzzling but even appropriate. So, recent philosophers have responded to Radford and have tried to demonstrate the rational explicability of fictional emotions. In Chapter Three I discuss two Reformist theories, set forth by Eva Schaper and Kendall Walton, which try to show that suitable beliefs *do* exist in the constitution of a fictional emotion. In Schaper's view fictional emotions are founded on 'second-order' beliefs about fictional characters and events. Second-order beliefs are appropriately formed once we have 'first-order' beliefs that the objects or events in question are fictional. Walton, on the other hand, wants to say that we '*make*-believe' in the actuality of fictional occurrences, and that these make-beliefs cause us to feel emotions towards fictional characters and events.

The main question I raise concerning the above theorists is whether their *extended* beliefs can be causally efficacious in evoking emotions. Does the notion of a make-belief or a second-order belief retain the generative power which is naturally possessed by a belief proper? My criticisms of both Schaper and Walton are directed towards establishing that, since their reformed or extended beliefs are reducible to pretended beliefs, the required causal efficacy cannot be attributed to these beliefs.

In Chapter Four I turn to the Radical theory, formulated by Roger Scruton, that our emotional responses to fictions are founded on a mental state or attitude essentially contrasted with belief, namely the imagination. The contrast is that whereas belief is a species of 'asserted' thought—a thought that carries existential commitment and can be assigned truth-values by reference to the actual world, not the world of stories—imagination is a species of 'unasserted' thought—a thought that is indifferent to truth or referential considerations and is merely entertained. Whereas suitable beliefs play their conceptual-cum-causal role in real-life emotions, the imagination fills that role in the occurrence of fictional emotions.

One question I deal with in connection with this theory is whether the imagination can be construed as invested with any causal efficacy to produce emotions of the type which are evoked by belief, *if* imagination and belief are held to be essentially contrasted. Secondly, if fictional emotions are necessarily continuous with real-life emotions—a thesis that the Radical theorist himself emphasizes— what accounts for the necessary continuity if the two emotions have essentially different causal conditions? I try to argue that the Radical theory fails to provide an adequate account that can accommodate proper answers to the above questions.

If neither make-belief nor second-order belief nor the imagination constitutes a proper causal condition of fictional emotions, we probably have to identify a legitimate place for belief proper in the structure of these emotions. But how is this possible in a fictional context? In Chapter Five I deal with this problem and propose my own solution in the form of what I entitle 'the Conservative theory'. I 'conserve' the standard view that suitable genuine beliefs form the foundation of emotions in general, and try to show that this is true, at least in part, of fictional emotions as well. My argument in its general form is that the thought process underlying fictional emotions is constituted neither by belief alone nor by the imagination alone, but by the interplay between the two.

Crucial to my argument is the distinction between existential belief and evaluative belief. Evidently there is no existential belief in the structure of a fictional emotion: the object is fictional. Hence the imagination plays the alternative role of representing the actuality of the fictional object. However, the evaluative belief, which is involved in the appreciation of the actual or analogous counterpart of the fictional object in emotion-relevant terms, remains as an essential ingredient of the fictional emotion in question. What is common between a particular fictional emotion and its real-life counterpart is the specific evaluative belief.

The evaluative belief is a sort of carrier of an 'image' of the normal emotional reality. When the intentional content provided by the imagination is brought under the purview of the suitable evaluative belief, the fictionality attached to the content is 'bracketed out'. The sense or significance borne by the content becomes the centre of attention, since the content is appreciated predominantly in the light of the emotional reality embodied in the evaluative belief. And as a carrier of an 'image' of the relevant emotional reality, this belief retains enough causal potency to be actualized even in its contact with a fictional context. A right kind of unasserted thought of the fictional object triggers off that causal dynamism. Thus the combination of imagination and evaluative belief results in a causally dynamic thought-complex, thereby eliciting what I have called 'fictional' emotions.

In the Conclusion I try to indicate the implications that my theory has for a wider understanding of the notion of fiction. I give a brief account of how my theory can explain why we value fiction as an exalted expression of human creativity and do not dismiss it as 'mere fiction'.

CHAPTER ONE

EMOTION AND BELIEF

1.1. INTENTIONALITY AS THOUGHT-DEPENDENCE: THINKING *OF* AND THINKING *THAT*

Franz Brentano's celebrated claim that intentionality—in the sense of object-directedness—is a mark of psychological phenomena can be explicated by reference to the notion of thought-dependence. Mental states in general, with the exception of some instances such as sensations and after-images, are directed towards their objects, that is what the states are about. Mental states are intentional arrows, so to speak, that necessarily hit on their respective targets. Hence the states essentially involve thoughts relating to these targets. And it is these thoughts that secure the object-directedness of states of mind. It is in this manner that the Brentano-thesis has been interpreted in contemporary analytical philosophy. For example, Richard Wollheim defends the thesis by paraphrasing it as 'the thesis that every mental state is identified by reference to a thought: a thought, that is, on the part of the person whose mental state it is'. (Wollheim, 1967–8, p. 1)

But the notion of a thought, or thought-dependence, needs to be made more definite, since there is no indication of whether the thought relating to an object is meant to be simply the thought *of* something or the thought *that* something is thus and so. For the difference between 'thinking *of*' and 'thinking *that*' is highly significant in so far as the nature of mental states is concerned. Clearly, not all thinking *of* is thinking *that,* although the converse is true. For example, if I think that X is F then it implies that I think of X's being F. But if I think of X's being F then it in no way implies that I assent to the proposition that X is F. For the state of affairs that I think of may be known to me to be entirely fictitious, so that my thought-process does not involve any readiness to assent to the statement describing the state of affairs. Therefore, 'thinking of' identifies a mental state quite different from the state identified by reference to 'thinking that'. As such, I shall adopt the following interpretation of the Brentano thesis, offered by Roger Scruton:

If there is a sense in which all mental states are essentially directed, then they will all involve the thought of an object. We might analyse the notion of 'thinking of' in terms of *entertaining* some proposition about the object, in which case we will have arrived at a conclusion congenial to the followers of Brentano, namely that a proposition (on 'intentional object') is involved in every mental state. (Scruton, 1971, p. 32)

Introducing the notion of 'entertaining' a proposition is, I think, a significant move in clarifying the thought-dependency interpretation of the intentionality thesis. To entertain a proposition *p* that concerns some object *O* is *merely* to think of *O*'s being thus and so. No existential commitment is thereby made about *O*'s actually satisfying the description given by *p*. Thus the entertaining of a proposition amounts to thinking about something in a non-judgemental state of mind—a state of mind that allows the thought to occur without involving referential or existential considerations. On the other hand, to think *that p* is, generally, to assert that something is the case. One is in a judgemental state of mind with regard to the object of thought, or the states of affairs represented by *p*, when one thinks *that p*. Judging is a mental act additional to that of entertaining a proposition with respect to the state of affairs that the proposition is about, namely the act of judging that the proposition is true.

It seems obvious that not all of our mental states involve judgemental thinking. To think about *X* is not necessarily to think *that X* is *F* or *G*, that is to judge that *X* is *F* or *G*. However, when we *do* think or judge that *X* is *F* (or *G*), it follows that we think of *X*'s being *F* (or *G*) *plus* the fact that we believe there to be an *X* which has the property *F* (or *G*). It is in this sense that thinking *that* something is the case logically presupposes thinking *of* something's being thus and so. And this points to the fact that thinking of something's being thus and so gives us the 'unjudged' or 'unasserted' version of the proposition which is asserted by virtue of the additional mental act of judging that it *is* thus and so. As such, the concept of 'thinking of' has logical priority over that of 'thinking that'. The former is wider in scope in that it covers all intentional states.

So far I have elucidated the distinction between 'thinking of' and 'thinking that' in terms of the concept of judgement and its overt counterpart, namely assertion. But what is essentially involved in the mental act of judging is believing. Believing is a necessary condition of judging, though believing, unlike judging, is dispositional or quasi-dispositional. In judging that something is thus and so one believes that the proposition in question is true: one gives assent to the proposition. Hence the concept of 'thinking that' embodies the concept of 'believing'; and believing is a propositional attitude contrasted with entertaining, or non-judgementally thinking about something. It is this doxastic attitude—the attitude of assent or belief to a proposition—the presence of which in some mental states distinguishes them from other mental states lacking this feature. Thus, 'thinking of' is a logical feature of those mental states that are unattached to the attitude of belief about the truth or falsity of what is thought about, or even the existence of the object of thought.

To put the point made above in a nutshell, not all intentional states involve belief about their objects. Not all thinking is believing, although what is thought in thinking about something is precisely what is believed in believing that the thing is (or is not) the case. For example, if I merely think of a gander chasing a goose, and then think or believe that a gander is chasing a goose, the contents of my thoughts in both cases are one and the same. It is the same proposition that represents both thought-contents. The difference is that in the former case the proposition is held in an attitude of mind indifferent to referential or existential considerations, while in the latter case it is held in an attitude of belief that concerns the truth of the proposition by reference to whether a gander is actually chasing a goose. Indeed, much of our thinking has the character of being indifferent to truth or belief. Hence it would be wrong to try to explain intentionality solely by reference to 'thinking that'. It is in the light of these considerations, I think, that Scruton's suggestion can be defended. Thus Scruton goes on to say that

it is by no means clear that all mental states—even if there is some sense in which they are all directed—involve the thought that something is the case. The paradigm of 'thinking that' is believing—a propositional attitude distinct from entertaining. And there seems to be a division among mental states between those which involve an element of belief (such as emotions and attitudes) and those (such as sensations and mental images) which do not. (Scruton, 1971, p. 32)

We may now broadly compartmentalize intentional states under 'thinking of' and 'thinking that'—merely thinking and believing. There seems to be a logical significance to this division in that 'thinking of' cannot be analysed in terms of 'thinking that', although all 'thinking that' presupposes 'thinking of'. Consider a sophisticated context of thought which can be schematically describable as 'thinking of *X* as *Y*', usually associated with the concept of 'seeing as' made familiar by Wittgenstein (Wittgenstein, 1953, part ii) and frequently discussed in the philosophy of perception.[1] For example, in seeing a particular figure in a picture as a woman bathing in a lake, the onlooker as it were thinks of the figure (X) as a woman (Y) engaged in a particular act, or lying in a particular posture. From this formulation it is not permissible to conclude that the onlooker actually sees (or thinks) *that X is Y*. He does not see or think that the picture-figure *is* a woman bathing in a lake: he merely sees or thinks of the figure *as* a woman engaged in bathing. Similarly, if I think of a mannequin as a nude woman, my thought-process in no way admits of legitimate analysis in terms of my thinking *that* the mannequin is a nude woman. There is no sense in which, while having this thought, I literally assert to myself that what I see *is* a nude woman. Thus thoughts of this kind irreducibly have the 'thinking of...' structure.[2]

Thus, mental states having the structure of 'thinking of X as Y' are to be subsumed under a mode of thought distinct from belief or judgement. The intentionality of such states is founded on thoughts that do not embody belief. Instead their intentionality rests on a complex thought which requires a *non-predicative* analysis. In having such a thought one is not just thinking about X but also about Y; for if is X's 'being' Y that one is thinking about. And it is precisely the complex thought of X's-being-Y that one cannot assert to oneself,

[1] Peter F. Strawson has discussed how the concept of *thinking-of-as* is related to Wittgenstein's notion of *seeing as*. See Strawson (1974), pp. 58–60.

[2] Metaphorical thinking in poetry also seems to fit the 'thinking of X as Y' structure. In Blake's mystical imagination, the thought of a finite *hour* evokes the thought of infinite *eternity* ('to see eternity in an hour...'); and his mystical vision of the *heaven* occurs at the sight of a *wild flower* ('and the heaven in a wild flower'). What Blake is implying, as it might be argued, is thinking *of* an hour as (or in terms of) eternity, and thinking *of* a wild flower as (or in terms of) the heaven. What he is not intending to imply is thinking *that* eternity is *in* an hour, or heavenliness is inherent in a mundane object such as a wild flower. In other words, it might be alleged that Blake's poetic thinking is not to be analysed as predicational: he does not think *that*...., but thinks *of* X as Y.

But, I think, this interpretation of poetic metaphor is likely to be misleading if it is meant to apply across the board. For a mystical poet like Blake might have had metaphysical beliefs of a pantheistic character. He might have believed that there is God or heavenliness in every finite and mundane object in an immanent form. Similarly, it might be a misrepresentation of Keat's thought expressed in his famous assertion 'Beauty is Truth, Truth Beauty' if we reinterpret the assertion as 'Beauty *as* Truth, Truth (*as*) Beauty'. For he might have held some quasi-mystical theory of the identity between Beauty and Truth.

or come to believe (literally) without absurdity. The thought of *Y* is *unpredicatively* attached to the thought of *X*—which is why it is impossible to formulate the thought in a that-clause. The existence of such psychological contexts, therefore, vindicates the need to divide the intentionality of mental states into 'thinking of . . .' and 'thinking that . . .'.

The 'thinking that . . .' construction allows the representation of states of mind that have the structure of predicational thought, e.g. 'something is thus and so'. This is not to imply that all thinking has the subject-predicate form and is about individuals, but only to indicate that there is a fundamental category of thought, expressed in declarative sentences, which involve reference to individuals and their properties, and has the above logical form. The subject of such sentences designates an object which is thought or judged (hence believed) to possess some property described by the predicate-expression—some property characteristic of the nature of the object. Hence, 'I think that *X* is *F*' permits 'I judge that *X* is *F*' or, when the inner act of judgement is expressed in the form of a public utterance, 'I assert that *X* is *F*'. The thought then is recognized as an 'asserted thought and is open to truth-conditional assessment. An asserted thought is, in essence, a thought which is cognized by the thinker to be true.[3]. In other words, the thought is believed to be true. Thus the paradigm of thinking that *X* is *F* is believing that '*X* is *F*' is true, and this reveals the close relationship between the mental disposition of belief and the overt act of assertion.

1.2 THE BELIEF-DEPENDENCE OF EMOTIONS

The foregoing account makes clear that there are mental states whose intentionality is essentially secured by unasserted thoughts. That is to say, the objects that such states are directed on to are identified by reference to thoughts which are not accompanied by the attitude of assent or belief. This category of mental states needs to be highlighted in order to compare and contrast it with another category, whose intentionality is secured by asserted thoughts, or thoughts that are tantamount to beliefs. In fact, it is a peculiarity of these mental states that they cannot be represented as what they

---

[3] Michael Dummett formulates the intimate link between assertion and truth in the following way: 'A man makes an assertion if he says something in such a manner as deliberately to convey the impression of saying it with the overriding intention of saying something true' (Dummett, 1973, p. 300).

essentially are without having recourse to the 'thinking that ...' construction. The thought embodied in such a state is such that the person, whose mental state it is, holds it to be true, or believes that there is a state of affairs in the world to which this thought in some way corresponds. So to identify this state is to refer to the thought *that X is F*—which is tantamount to the belief that *X* is *F*. Thus there is no way of characterizing the real essence or identity of such a state apart from referring to the belief that there is something of which some property holds true. It is the suitable belief about the object that determines the 'direction' of this mental state towards the object. And if the belief is somehow removed or altered, that state of mind will also be correspondingly made to disappear or modified. The intentional link between the state and the object will be severed.

It has been the view of many philosophers that emotions are such belief-dependent, judgemental mental states.[4] They argue that the analysis of an emotion necessarily involves reference to the subject's thought or belief about the object of the emotion. And it is this belief that is said to secure the intentionality or object-directedness of the emotion, such that the belief or thought is foundational to the existence of the emotion.

Now, perhaps this thesis is not true if it is intended to account for the entire range of emotions. For it is not at all clear whether emotions form a natural class so that each member can be seen as belonging to a homogeneous group. Some philosophers have pointed out that emotions should be taken to form a heterogeneous group, so that they cannot all be shepherded together under one set of classifications as thought-generated, thought-defined or belief-dependent.[5] Furthermore, there are many experiences which are infused with emotional 'charge' or feeling. Consider, for example, the feeling that one has in watching a sunset on a lovely summer evening. One is then experiencing a delightful feeling. It does not seem appropriate to explain the occurrence of this feeling by reference to any belief about the sunset. Similarly, when one feels awe at the sight of an ocean or a mountain, there seems to be no belief that can be cited in the explanation of one's emotional state. Presumably, the same thing can be said with regard to vague and inexplicable

---

[4] For example, Alston (1967), Bedford (1956-7), Gordon (1974), Green (1972), Kenny (1963), Lyons (1980), Neu (1977), Scruton (1970–1), Shaffer (1983), Solomon (1977), Taylor (1975) and Thalberg (1964).

[5] For example, see Rorty (1980), p. 1.

feelings of depression or *angst,* which appear to be based on no particular belief.

However, the belief-dependency thesis holds as an explanation of emotions if we make a distinction between emotions *proper* and moods and other affectively charged attitudes. By 'emotions proper' I mean those emotions for which we have common names, as both Taylor (Taylor, 1975, p. 391) and Hanfling (Hanfling, 1983, p. 241) point out. We may think of fear, anger, jealousy, pride, pity, grief, indignation, remorse, regret, gratitude as cases of such emotions.[6] And it would not be wrong to say that we account for most of the major human emotions when we go through the ones listed above. The intentionality or object-directedness of these emotions is describable by reference to specific beliefs with regard to the respective objects. The intentional structure of such an emotion is such that without the belief in question the occurrence of the emotion will be unaccountable. I could not feel regretful about myself if I did not believe that I was the agent of some past misconduct. You cannot be angry with your enemy without believing that the enemy has done some harm to you. A person feels grateful to another person because the former believes that the latter has done something valuable or important to him. Similarly, Othello could not have been jealous of Desdemona without having the belief that she was involved in an intimate affair with Cassio. It is in this sense that to attribute an emotion of the above kind and to deny the characteristic belief is to deny the emotion—which means that the appropriate beliefs are foundational to the existence of emotions of this category.

Concerning any emotion of this category, it will be impossible to identify the emotion if no reference is made to the suitable belief the subject holds about what the emotional state is directed on to. If a person S feels an emotion E towards some object or event X, then the explanation of the occurrence of E roughly takes the following form: S feels E because S believes (or thinks) that X is F, where F designates some emotion-evoking property characteristically possessed by X. Necessarily, S believes that X exists or occurs,

[6] O. H. Green makes the same cautious move when he begins his essay with this statement: 'Beliefs of certain sorts are characteristic of the several emotions.' He then adds to the above a footnote remark: 'Application of the term "emotion" is throughout restricted to a range of conative-affective states including embarrassment, pity, grief, indignation, fear, remorse, and other quite similar examples' (Green, 1972, p. 24).

Gabriele Taylor also restricts the belief-dependency thesis to a particular class of emotions. See Taylor (1975–6).

and also believes that F is true of X. It may be that F is not, in point of fact, true of X, i.e. that S is mistaken in believing that X is F. Nevertheless, the belief that X is true of F is a necessary component of the total mental state E. Even the belief that X exists may be mistaken, when there is no corresponding 'real' object denoted by 'X'. But the belief that X exists also remains as a necessary component of E. Thus the intentional nexus between E and X is sustained by the evaluative belief that X is F, combined with the existential belief that the object designated by 'X' exists. Hence, if S discovers or comes to realize that it is not F but G which is true of X, and F and G are incompatible with one another, this evaluative belief will be replaced by some evaluative belief appropriate to X. In consequence, the original nexus will be broken to give rise to a new intentional nexus. And similarly if S finds out that X does not exist, E will begin to disappear or be replaced by some other mental state.

For example, were Othello to be convinced that Desdemona had not been involved in an intimate affair with Cassio and that the apparent evidence to the contrary was due to the machinations of Iago, his jealousy would disappear. Of course there is no guarantee that the discovery of the falsity of his belief that his wife is unfaithful to him will automatically or immediately result in a state of mind totally unperturbed by the previous feeling. However, given his new belief, Othello can no longer be simply or straightforwardly jealous. At best the jealousy will soon be over, and at worst, if the thought of Desdemona's unfaithfulness somehow continues, his jealousy might continue in the form of a perturbed mental state that can be described as pathological jealousy. Thus the change of the relevant belief leads to a corresponding change in the emotion attached to the belief, which in turn requires a redescription of the resultant mental state. The resultant state of mind must be redescribed because the original state of mind, namely jealousy, essentially involved Othello's belief that Desdemona was unfaithful to him. He can no longer be said to be jealous, though he may well still be in turmoil.

Thus far the foregoing arguments have been adduced to substantiate the thesis that intentionality of emotions, understood in the circumscribed sense of the term, is secured by reference to belief. However, it might be alleged that a person can know that something is the case, yet not believe it, and still feel a particular emotion in spite of the lack of the suitable belief. For example, someone might argue that a young woman can come to know that she has cancer, yet not believe it, but still suffer from anxiety. The question then is whether her anxiety is directed towards the cancer. If it is, the apparent puzzle would be: How could she be anxious that she has cancer when she disbelieves that she has cancer? What is it that her anxiety is founded on if the belief appropriate to her mental state is held to be absent? What secures the intentionality of her anxiety?

Emotional states of this kind are described as self-deceptive emotions. Such cases are complicated and deserve careful analysis. The crux of the problem in the above example is how the woman is involved in a complex process of deceiving herself into a state of disbelief about what she knows. For it seems that to know that *p* and still not believe that *p* is tantamount to denying that one knows that *p*. In the face of such a self-contradiction, her case can perhaps be construed as her unwillingness to avow or acknowledge explicitly what she implicitly claims to know. She is unwilling to reconcile her knowledge about her incurable illness with her general attitude to life or her health, namely the desire to live longer, or to avoid painful suffering.

But, I think, it is not that she really does not assent to the knowledge-claim. Rather, she somehow succeeds in blinding herself to what she already believes to be true. For it is quite plausible to think that her engaging in a psychological strategy to transmute a belief, which threatens her life, into a disbelief, is precisely what creates inner tension in her. For a permanent success would imply that the reason for, and cause of, being anxious had been completely eliminated from her mind. The inadequacy of her defensive psychological strategy results in the resuscitation of the buried belief. The belief that she *has* cancer reasserts itself.

But, then, it now appears as though it is the struggle to replace the belief with its opposite disposition, rather than the belief itself, which is the cause of, or reason for, her anxiety. The intentionality of her anxiety seems to consist in a conflict of beliefs or dispositions. If this is true, we again confront the problem of not being able to provide an account of the intentionality of this mental state in accordance with our theory. For no determinate belief would be adduced in explaining the anxiety. Is there any ambivalence about her mental state?

Against this possible consequence, I want to argue that the belief that she has cancer, accompanied by the evaluative belief that cancer will bring an end to her life through painful suffering, secures the intentionality of her anxiety. For her disbelief is less well-grounded than her belief; the strength of her belief keeps her disbelief from gaining a secure ground. In essence, her disbelief is her unwillingness to recognize the belief. And the persistence of her anxiety is due to the persistence and dominance of her belief, which is why her strategy fails to obtain more than a transient success.

1.3. THE FORMAL OBJECT OF EMOTIONS

To say that an emotion is founded on an appropriate belief is to imply that the belief characteristic of the emotion concerns the object that the emotion is directed on to. But the intentional nexus that binds an emotion to its object deserves elaborate analysis in view of the fact that there are conceptual restrictions on the type of object which each emotion could have. In talking about the relation between emotion and object one must understand that the word 'object' is being used in a formal or logical sense as opposed to a material or empirical sense, such that the relationship between it and the relevant emotion is itself logical or conceptual. Not just anything can be the object of a particular emotion. For the object of an emotion is the object of an appropriate belief; it is an object specified by the belief as possessed of certain property. Each of the emotions is logically appropriate to certain objects satisfying the descriptions given by appropriate beliefs. Thus the person having the emotion must believe that the object falls under a certain description characteristic of the emotion. The description uniquely identifies the object of the emotion: one can feel the emotion E only if one sees the object O as fitting the description D. Since fitting the description D is a formal requirement which the object O must satisfy for E to occur, it is argued that emotions (and actions) have 'formal objects'—a medieval phrase of Aristotelian provenance, recently applied to the discussion of intentionality by Anthony Kenny. (Kenny 1963) Kenny introduces the idea of a formal object through an analysis of actions:

> The formal object of $\emptyset$ is the object under the description which *must* apply to it if it is possible to $\emptyset$ it. If only what is P can be $\emptyset$ed, then 'thing which is P' gives the formal object of $\emptyset$ing.... To assign a formal object to an action is to place restrictions on what may occur as the direct object of a verb describing the action. (Kenny, 1963, p. 189)

For instance, if one can borrow only what belongs to somebody else, then 'belonging to others' is a description of the formal object of borrowing. If one can strive only for what is difficult to obtain, then 'being difficult to obtain' is the description of the formal object of striving. Whatever it is that can be borrowed must be something which is believed to belong to somebody else. Whatever it is that can be striven for must be something which the agent believes to be difficult to obtain. Thus, the formal objects of actions specify conceptual restrictions on what can be counted as this or that particular action.

Actions are both intentional (thought-dependent) and non-intentional. Even non-intentional actions are specified by their formal objects. Touching and drinking are non-intentional actions and are specified by their formal objects. Only what is tangible can be touched; only what is liquid can be drunk. But in neither case does the agent have to believe that the object he is touching is tangible, or that the object he is drinking is liquid. And these two activities are not object-directed. Water, for instance, is an 'object' to drink. But drinking a glass of water is not analysable in terms of the drinking being directed on to the glass of water. Similarly, when I touch the pen while writing this sentence my act of touching is not said to be directed on to the pen. Of course, my *intending* or *desiring* to touch the pen is directed on to the pen. In that case it is not the pen *tout court* but the pen as intended or desired—as believed to possess some quality because of which I intend or desire to touch it.

Actions that have the property of intentionality are such that they cannot be counted as what they are independently of the agent's belief about their objects. I cannot be said to borrow a car if I do not believe that it belongs to somebody else. The act of borrowing necessarily involves being in a definite mental state—a state that embodies the thought that the object pertains to someone else. So it is not something pertaining to someone else *tout court,* but something *believed* to be pertaining to someone else that is the formal object of borrowing. The formal object of an intentional action is thus determined by reference to an appropriate belief. It is the belief which secures the intentionality of the action.

The intentionality of actions parallels the intentionality of emotions. The formal objects of emotions are specified in much the same way in which the formal objects of intentional actions are specified. Just as, for instance, only what is believed to be difficult to obtain can be striven for, so only what is believed to be a valuable achievement or possession of oneself can be an object of pride. Likewise, only what is believed to be good or desirable and believed to belong to somebody else can be envied. Again *A* can be jealous of *B* only if *A* believes that *B* has been preferred in some way to himself. Only what is believed to be a great loss or misfortune can be an object of grief. In each case, the formal object specifies, and thereby puts conceptual restrictions on, the *kind* of object (actual or fictitious) on to which the particular emotion can be directed. An emotion is logically, not just ethically, appropriate only to certain restricted objects—this is thus a formal condition which must be satisfied by the emotion in order to be that emotion.

However, to say that assigning a formal object to an emotion places a restriction on the kind of object towards which one can have the emotion is not to imply that one cannot, for example, be envious or jealous or proud of anything whatsoever. In point of fact, what is necessary for the possibility of experiencing an emotion is the appropriate belief or thought *that* something is the case. For the restriction put by the formal object concerns not the object *per se* but the appropriate belief about the object. For example, although the formal object of pride is the possession of something which casts credit on oneself, I may take pride in something which does not really cast any credit on myself in that it is not connected to myself. This can happen if I mistakenly believe it to be connected with myself. You may feel fear at the appearance of a robin redbreast because you may believe its appearance to be ominous. Likewise,

it is possible to be envious of one's own fruit trees; but only if one mistakenly believes that the land on which they stand is part of one's neighbour's property; just as it is possible to feel remorse for the failure of the crops in Vietnam if one believes that it was due to the inadequacies of one's own prayers. (Kenny, p. 193)

The rationale behind the above discussion is that what the formal object designates with respect to an emotion must be understood to qualify only the intentional object—i.e. the object as believed. The formal object specifies a limitation not on the material object of the emotion, but on the thought through which the material object is presented. This also partly explains why one can fear something that actually does not exist, or feel delighted at something which did not really happen—or happened in a way different from the way it was thought to have happened. A mistaken or false emotion is an emotion founded on a mistaken belief about its object. Having the emotion is no guarantee that its formal object is always accompanied by an instance of what it designates. For there may not exist any material or real instance; and even if there is one, it may not be as the designation requires it to be.

The above can be contrasted with the description of actions that are not characterized by intentionality. What the formal object of such an action designates cannot but qualify the material object, for the relation between the action and its object is a material (non-intentional) relation. Kenny writes:

> The description of the formal object of a mental attitude such as an emotion, unlike the description of the formal object of a non-intentional action, must contain reference to belief. Only what is wet can be dried; but something which is merely believed to be an insult may provoke anger. (Kenny, pp. 193–4)

Two interrelated features can be brought to light on the basis of the above elucidation. One is that an emotion is *founded* on an appropriate belief (the feature of intentionality); the other is that the belief is *causally efficacious* in bringing about the emotional state in the subject (the feature of causation). Faced with the need to classify emotions as of particular types, we would invoke the feature of intentionality. For example, we would classify an emotion as one of fear or of anger or of jealousy in terms of the particular type of beliefs involved in each case. And faced with the need to answer the question 'What makes you angry with or jealous of him/her?' we would respond by resorting to the feature of causation. That is, we would say, not just that he/she has done some harm to us or prefers someone else to us in some respect, but that we believe this to be the case and are emotionally affected *because* of what we believe.

It is pertinent to emphasize that the belief on which an emotion is founded is not just a purely cognitive, descriptive or factual belief—a belief of the kind which is claimed to be involved in a paradigm perceptual judgement. Although the initial judgement, that the object of the emotion possesses some property characteristic of the emotion, contains a factual or descriptive belief about existence, it is also the basis for an evaluation, and it is this evaluation which transforms the initial cognitive and factual attitude into a specific way of viewing the object. For example, if I feel terror at the sight of a raging bull bearing down on me, I am not merely aware of the fact that the object has such and such properties, but realize that those properties constitute the object's being dangerous to my existence.

The raging bull is seen *as* a threatening object which can injure or kill me. Likewise, a man is angry because a situation is seen by him *as* offensive or insulting, embarrassed because a situation is seen *as* one in which he has lost face. Thus the belief or judgement on which the emotion is founded is an *evaluative* belief or judgement—involving an appraisal of the object or situation. As William Lyons points out,

> we will only count this emotional state as a case of fear if the person's particular judgements, say, that there is a bomb in the corner of the room and that it is likely to injure or kill him, are judgements which together can be said to fall under the general category or description of viewing the situation as dangerous. (Lyons, 1980, p. 78)

This explanation ties up well with the idea of a formal object. For to claim that a person is in the emotional state of fear is to imply that the person must view the object in a certain light—namely, as dangerous, harmful, unpleasant or disagreeable—and that the general category summing up this particular point of view for fear, that is the category of being dangerous, harmful, disagreeable (a disjunction of these properties), is the formal object of fear.[7]

1.4. GENERAL EVALUATIVE BELIEF AND PARTICULAR EXISTENTIAL BELIEF

Since to assign a formal object to an emotion is to state the general evaluative category of objects or situations the emotion must be

---

[7] So far I have related my discussion of the notion of a formal object of emotion to analytic philosophers only. But the idea that an emotion has a formal object is also to be found in the writings of some representatives of both phenomenological philosophy and cognitive psychology, where the idea has been elucidated in a much more general sense and from a broader perspective. If the formal object of an emotion is to be construed as 'object-as-evaluated' by the person having the emotion, then we are permitted to generalize that our emotional responses to the world of objects and events are determined by, and classified in accordance with, the way we evaluate the various properties possessed by the objects and events. Thus, Jean Paul Sartre says that 'emotion is a specific way of apprehending the world' (Sartre, 1962, p. 57). And it is implied that our responding to a certain segment of the world with a particular emotion is due to our believing evaluatively that the segment is invested with some specific quality appropriate to the generation of that emotion. 'Emotion is not an accident, it is a mode of our conscious existence, one of the ways in which consciousness understands (in Heideggar's sense of *verstehen*) its Being-in-the-world' (Sartre, p. 31). In a similar vein of mind, a contemporary psychologist, Richard Lazarus, says: 'Emotion results from an evaluative perception of a relationship (actual, imagined or anticipated) between a person (or animal) and the environment' (Lazarus, 1982, p. 1021).

about, it is obvious that no particular object or situation has thereby been assigned to the emotion. It merely states what *type* of object or situation something must be for it to be an object of the emotion. Correspondingly, the general evaluative belief appropriate to the emotion is not specifically about any particular object or situation, but about objects or situations of a certain kind. A formal object, being an evaluative category and determined by a suitable general belief, is a generalization, a type description. Strictly speaking, a formal object is not an *object* but a concept or conceptual framework which is applied to particular objects or situations. It is an evaluative framework constituted of certain evaluative criteria which are provided by the relevant general belief. The particular object or situation which is made to fit that conceptual framework is, as we might say, the 'material' object of the emotion. Thus we also assign a material object to an emotion, which means that we refer to a particular spatio-temporal item (given that there is one) that the subject is emotional about.

Take the examples of sadness and envy. A person feels sadness towards another if the former believes that the latter is a victim of some misfortune, whether of health or family problem or socio-political pressures of some kind. Then the concept of 'being a victim of some misfortune' sets the framework by reference to which a person's condition is deemed saddening. Thus we feel sadness towards a poor and innocent village blacksmith when we believe that some despicable vandalism has smashed his workplace, leaving him with no means of livelihood. We see the blacksmith's lot fitting the framework that explains when a situation can be saddening. Similarly, the framework for our finding a fellow human being's life, or a specific condition of that life, enviable is set by the belief that this person is better off than we are in some respect that is considered good. Thus the runner-up tennis player envies the champion because he believes that the champion has obtained something which he failed to obtain, namely the championship trophy or money and/or the fame.

This distinction between a 'formal object' and a 'material object' of an emotion can be fruitfully used to elicit a corresponding distinction on the side of belief, namely a 'general (evaluative) belief' and a 'particular (existential) belief' respectively. While the formal object is related to an appropriate general belief in that the latter determines the former, the material object of an emotion also relates itself to a belief, namely the belief that there exists this particular item on to which the emotion in question is directed. Thus, if Mary is feeling fear at the sight of a wild dog approaching her, she not only believes that wild dogs can harm her in certain ways; she also believes in the actual presence of a particular wild dog confronting her. An explanation of her fear must attribute both these beliefs to her. For her fear not only has a formal object but a material object as well, which figures as an instantiation of the category of objects thought to be harmful or dangerous.

Now, it might appear that the two beliefs are not always necessary for someone to feel an emotion like fear. For there are cases of fear in the explanation of which the relevant existential belief does not, at first sight, seem to be attributed to the subject. Consider the cases of recollection and anticipation. Mary may simply remember a wild dog running towards her and feel fear at that. Or she may, rather obsessively, anticipate an attack and thereby feel fear. It might then be said that in neither case does Mary hold the existential belief in a wild dog threatening her while she is in her fearful state of mind: only the general evaluative belief about wild dogs is operative in her frightened consciousness, and thus only this belief is logically involved in the concept of fear in general. Hence the conclusion might be drawn that the general evaluative belief about something dangerous or harmful is by itself necessary and sufficient to produce fear.

This argument, however, is fallacious. What the cases of recollection and obsessive anticipation actually imply is not that Mary's fear is founded on no existential belief whatsoever, but that it occurs in the absence of the belief in a currently existing wild dog. In other words, there is an existential belief of a relatively different kind that is operative in the generation of Mary's fear, namely the belief in the past or possible existence, or appearance, of a wild dog running towards her. The point to be drawn from this is that the general evaluative belief involved in an emotion is always in need of some other mental act or state to be actually effective in eliciting the emotion. When it is not accompanied by an existential belief about a currently existing object, or an occurrent event, it is accompanied by some substitute thought-process, such as memory or anticipation, that embodies existential beliefs in different ways. This is to say that statements about emotions generated through recollection and anticipation entail existential commitments of different sorts than those which are entailed by statements about perceptually generated emotions. We might say that the general belief is ignited when the mental process of recollection or anticipation, involving the belief in past or possible existence of the object, is turned on.

It should be noted that the difference in existential commitments involved in different modes of emotions discussed above corresponds to differences in action or behaviour resulting from the emotions. If Mary feels fear at the *sight* of a wild dog running towards her, she will normally tend to avoid the dangerous situation either by running away from the dog or by obstructing its progress towards her, which is to say that her fear will issue in some appropriate immediate action. When such an action actually issues. it can be connected with her belief in a currently existing dangerous object facing her. On the other hand, if she feels fear at the *thought* of a wild dog attacking her, the fear will normally not be accompanied by the desire or motive to engage in the appropriate immediate action mentioned above. But she may be *disposed* to behave in certain ways and undergo some physiological changes that are characteristic of fear. In other words, her fear will be expressed in certain passive symptoms, or in reactions without actions of the appropriate kind. This fact can be connected with the (existential) belief that the wild dog is not currently threatening her, but it was threatening her or could do so in future. But in either case the evaluative belief remains the same.

There is a further reason why the distinction between general evaluative belief and particular existential belief has a significant conceptual role to play in accounting for the transformation or cessation of emotional states. For instance, a man might harbour the general belief about a species of animal in a particular forest that such an animal is a devil which comes to carry people off. Upon encountering a particular animal of that species while wandering by that forest, he would feel afraid that the animal is a threat to his life. But if somehow he could be convinced that this general belief concerning such animals of that forest is nothing but a baseless superstition, he would cease, or at any rate begin to cease, to see the animal—which he believes to be approaching him—as a threatening or devilish object. His existential belief about the animal would no longer be governed by his initial evaluative belief about animals of that species residing in that forest. His existential commitment to the particular object would, so to speak, be free from the existential anxiety which he suffered earlier on. Thus, the kind of influence which the existential belief would have on the subject is completely determined by what general belief reigns over it.

1.5 THE NON-CONTINGENT CAUSAL CONNECTION BETWEEN EMOTION AND BELIEF

It has been held that a suitable belief about the object of an emotion is not only conceptually necessary for the emotion to be what it is, but is also causally efficacious in producing that emotion. (Davidson, 1982; Green, 1972; Lyons, 1980; Neu, 1977) So the relationship between emotion and belief has two dimensions—conceptual and causal. The conceptual dimension is the *rational* aspect of the link: the belief on which the emotion is founded is the reason for that emotion. At the same time, it is because of the belief that the subject feels that emotion—the 'because' here being causal. Since the same mental phenomenon is being explained in terms of both a conceptual and a causal connection, it is necessary to argue for the idea that causal connections do not preclude conceptual connections, and vice versa. It needs to be explained how beliefs can play a causal role in belief-dependent states, even though belief-dependency is generally a matter of the classification and discrimination of mental states and is, therefore, a conceptual matter.

If a relation to a certain belief is a logically necessary condition of an emotion's being the emotion it is, then it will be readily questioned how the relationship between the two can be held to be causal. For the belief is a defining characteristic of the emotion and, hence, is a constituent of it. But if the belief and the emotion are to be construed as cause and effect respectively, the belief must be shown to be a separate event—an event that can be identified independently of the emotion. This objection is raised by Irving Thalberg, who contends that a causal relation between X and Y presupposes that the two events, X and Y, are independently describable. He states:

It seems to me that any time you claim one event or condition is a cause or condition of another event or condition, you must be able to gather evidence of the effect which is logically independent of your evidence of its putative cause. (Thalberg, 1964, p. 51)

Put in general terms, Thalberg's argument is that if having an emotion necessarily implies having the appropriate belief—a statement which entails that one cannot gather evidence of the emotion (effect) that is logically independent of one's evidence of the belief (cause)—then the principle of logical independence is violated in saying that the characteristic belief causes the emotion in question.

What underlies the above argument is a general philosophical principle, essentially Humean in spirit, that a logical or conceptual

connection precludes a causal connection—a principle which has
been much criticized in recent philosophy. (See, for example,
Davidson, 1963, and Wilson, 1972, Chapters 2 and 3.) Against
this principle, J.R.S. Wilson puts forward the thesis that causal
connection is built into the meaning of certain concepts. He writes:

Sometimes two concepts are related in that any item which falls under one
has a certain relation to some item falling under the other. Thus any item
falling under the concept father has a certain relation to some item falling
under the concept child; any item falling under the concept cause has a
certain relation to some item falling under the concept effect. (Wilson,
1972, p. 25)

This general counter-thesis to the Humean principle has been advocated in more specific terms by O.H. Green, who thinks Thalberg
and others have overlooked the fact that

many descriptions are applicable only where a certain causal relation is
supposed to hold. The causal relation is built into the meaning of such
descriptions. Where this is the case, the fact that a logical connection
obtains will not preclude the existence of a causal connection. For example,
a burn is by definition an injury caused by contact with heat; thus, where
there is a burn, of course there is contact with heat, but this hardly means
that contact with heat is not the cause of the burn. (Green, p. 38)

Green then goes on to argue that emotion words are similarly
analysable. For an emotion is partially defined as 'an affective state
caused by a thought of a certain sort' (*ibid.*). 'Fear', for example, is
partially defined as an affective state caused by the anticipation of
some danger.

   I think that the Green-Wilson argument is persuasive. The conceptual connection of an emotion of a certain sort with a belief of a
specific kind does not preclude the belief causing the emotion, any
more than the conceptual constraints on 'fathers', 'effect' and
'burns' precludes their being causally related to 'sons' and 'causes'
and 'contact with heat'. The causal relation in the case of emotions
can be exhibited by analysing the total mental state of an emotion
into its constituent parts. Basically an emotion consists of two units:
first, a cognitive-evaluative aspect, which is the aspect of belief;
second, an affective aspect consisting of certain sensational and
physiological states. The affective aspect is generally linked with
characteristic behaviours or actions in which the whole emotional
state expresses itself. Now the affective aspect, or the occurrence of
certain unusual or abnormal physiological changes associated with

adrenaline flow, blood circulation, respiration, muscular tension, gastro-intestinal activity, secretions—in short, those changes associated with the central nervous system—must be causally accounted for, let alone the behaviours or actions in which the emotion is manifested. Since the belief-component is the only other constituent of the total emotional complex, it seems necessary to refer to the belief in providing a causal explanation of the observable physiological/sensational effects.[8] Thus, even if the belief is a logically essential constituent of the emotion, it is plausible to say that the belief causes the emotion in so far as the affective reaction is elicited by that belief. But exactly how this type of causation operates is the next question we must address.

The most likely suspicion with respect to the feasibility of causation of some affective reaction by a belief is that the antecedent of this network is not an event to be related to the consequent. A belief is not an event but an attitude or disposition (although it could become an event by being an occurrent belief). And for the belief to become an event the subject has to bring it to the threshold of his consciousness, or it has to occur there and persist somewhat like an obsessive thought. However, this is not normally how our emotions are related to their appropriate beliefs. The occurrence of fear, for example, is not so much accompanied by the simultaneous or prior occurrence of the belief that something is dangerous, as it is triggered off by the disposition to behave in a way characteristic of fear when faced with the dangerous object. So the belief is active not as an occurrent state of mind but in the form of a disposition. Yet not being an event, how can a belief be said to bring about another event?

The above perplexity arises, however, from a failure to recognize the complex belief-structure of emotions. It is true that the evaluative belief need not be a mental occurrence, even when an account of it

---

[8] William Lyons suggests that the link between emotion and evaluative belief is to be construed as causal for 'modified Humean reasons'. As he writes:

If it is known, as it is, that physiological changes of the type we are concerned with do often follow on the generation or activation of some evaluative disposition in a person, and if in a certain case the physiological changes follow quite directly the evaluation, and if it is known that there is nothing else present in or near the person who is undergoing these physiological changes which might be associated with these changes, then one has good reasons for claiming that the evaluation is the cause of the physiological changes. It is quite simply a matter of the evaluation being the best claimant in the circumstances for being the cause of the observed physiological effects. (Lyons, pp. 61–2)

is given in relation to emotions as occurrent states. A dispositional analysis of the evaluative belief can be correct. But if the evaluative belief involved in a particular emotion is to play a causal role in occurrent emotional states, there must be some occurrent aspect to this belief. It seems necessary to posit some factor, psychological or physiological, which actually exists, in some sense, in the subject. In other words, the disposition has some sort of structural or categorical—as opposed to hypothetical or non-actual—base in the subject. Just as, for instance, there is a physico-chemical structural base of a material disposition like brittleness or magnetism, so there must be a dynamic psycho-physiological structure underlying the evaluative belief. It is this dynamic structural base which renders the belief causally efficacious in eliciting an emotion.

But we have not yet fully answered the question of how a disposition actually plays the role of a causal operator in generating a certain emotion. For merely to say that a suitable evaluative belief is the cause of an emotion, in the way brittleness is the cause of the breaking of a glass jar, is not to provide a complete explanation. Although the disposition of brittleness is a causal factor in the breaking of the glass jar, it does not constitute a sufficient condition for the jar to break. Some other condition, such as the jar's falling on rocky ground, has to be added to produce a sufficient explanation. All we have so far is a necessary condition of the occurrence of the event.

The sufficient condition can be provided, I think, by bringing in the role of the existential belief. The existential belief is always an occurrent mental state, and its occurrence normally triggers off the disposition to feel or behave in a certain way appropriate to the relevant evaluative belief. The relevant disposition is 'actualized' by virtue of a mental occurrence of the instantaneous variety. Thus the functional role of the existential belief in an emotion is analogous to the role of striking a glass jar by some hard substance in breaking the jar. And it is in this way, I think that the belief component of an emotional complex is activated to become an event of some sort.

1.6. SUMMARY

In this chapter I have tried to analyse the notion of intentionality or object-directedness of mental states by reference to the concepts of 'thinking of' and 'thinking that'. While 'thinking of' is representative of unasserted thoughts, or thoughts merely entertained or held in a non-judgemental state of mind, the paradigm of 'thinking that' is believing, or asserted thoughts—thoughts that are held in a judgemental state of mind. The distinction is intended to draw a general demarcation between thinking *without* believing and thinking *as* believing. I have explained the intentionality of emotional states of a certain kind in terms of 'thinking that' or belief. Emotions of this category are belief-dependent: they are founded on, and hence identified by reference to, appropriate beliefs. And the appropriate belief specifies what is called the 'formal object' of an emotion. The 'formal object' of a certain emotion is given by a description under which an object or situation must be believed to fall if it is to be the object of that emotion. This description is about the general evaluative category under which a 'material' object must be subsumed if it is to be the object of the emotion in question.

In view of the importance and complexity of the belief-structure of emotions, I have drawn a distinction between general evaluative beliefs and particular existential beliefs. The evaluative belief involved in a certain emotion consists of an evaluative judgement about the nature of the object, that is some belief that the object possesses such-and-such emotion-evoking property. The existential belief consists of the judgement or belief that there is such an object or situation possessing the property specified by the evaluative belief.

I then argued for the thesis that the non-contingent or conceptual relation between emotion and belief is also a causal relation. Emotions are not merely defined and classified in terms of appropriate beliefs; the beliefs are also causally efficacious in generating the relevant emotions. Finally, I have explained how this causation actually takes place. Although the evaluative belief is analysable as a disposition to feel or behave in a certain way appropriate to the belief, the existential belief is a mental occurrence that triggers off the disposition and causes a particular type of affective experience. Thus the belief-component of a total emotional complex, consisting of both the evaluative and the existential belief, provides a necessary and sufficient causal explanation of the occurrence of emotions.

CHAPTER TWO

RATIONALITY, BELIEF
AND EMOTIONAL RESPONSE
TO FICTION

2.1 THE PARADOX OF FICTIONAL EMOTION

Not only do we give a causal explanation of the occurrence of an emotion by reference to an appropriate belief, we also provide a rational explanation of it by citing the same belief as the reason for someone's being in that state. In the previous chapter our discussion was mainly concerned with the causal dimension. In the present chapter I shall probe the role of belief in the rational dimension. My aim, however, is not to deal with the general problem of the rationality of emotions. It is to examine the rationality of a specific category of emotions which has attracted attention in recent philosophy, namely our emotional response to fiction.

Philosophers have found the phenomenon of an emotional response to fiction conceptually troublesome. They are perplexed as to how the occurrence of such an emotion—which I shall entitle 'fictional emotion' in comparison and contrast with real-life emotions—is to be accounted for by reference to belief. For if the intentionality of emotions is determined by suitable beliefs, what is the belief (or beliefs) which I hold about a fictional character or situation and which I am supposed to cite as the reason for and cause of my feeling a certain emotion towards the character or situation? If I feel sad about Anna Karenina or Desdemona, then it should imply that I believe that the woman in question has undergone, or is undergoing, some misfortune. Without this belief my emotional response would seem to be without any (rational) foundation. But is it *rationally* possible for me to form this belief in my clear awareness that the woman to whom I respond with sadness is *fictional*? And how could anyone respond to the fictional woman with an emotion which normally presupposes the subject's having an appropriate belief about the nature and existence of the object? How could anyone rationally take the fictional as factual *to the extent that* one is thereby affectively moved in much the same way as one would be moved if it were real?

From the rational standpoint, what someone believes in attending to a fictional object or situation is that it is *fictional*—a creation of the imagination. The attentive process of the subject occurs under the concept of fiction. Evidently, then, the rational possibility of existential commitment to the object or situation is logically excluded, so that there is nothing existential to respond to. On the other hand, forming the appropriate belief on which a certain emotion is founded requires that one also believe in the actual or possible existence of the object or event to which one responds. What follows from this is that the tribunal of rationality announces the impossibility of fictional emotions.

However, the adjudication of rationality seems to be challenged by facts about human reaction to fictions. For it is a plain fact of human emotional life that we often go to watch plays, films and operas, or read novels and observe paintings; and often our natural reaction to various fictional performances and scenes is that of becoming emotional about fictional persons and events. In spite of our knowledge that a certain character or scene is part of a fictitious account, we are easily moved by it. So it naturally opens up the perplexing question: How can our being aware of the fictionality of what we attend to be consistent with our reacting to it as if we are attending to something real? Is there not a cognitive dissonance underlying our emotional response to fiction?

It has been suspected that the problem of fictional emotions is that they involve a paradox about belief. To describe this paradox, I can do no better than quote Peter Lamarque's succinct presentation of it:

On the one hand, it is assumed that as reasonably sophisticated adults, we are not *taken in* by fiction; that is, we do not believe or come to believe, when knowingly watching a fictional performance, that the depicted sufferings or dangers involve any real suffering or danger. No one is in fact murdered in the performance of *Othello*, just as no one is in fact jealous or innocent. And we know that. On the other hand, we respond often enough with a range of emotions, including fear and pity, that seem to be explicable only on the assumption that we do after all believe there to be real suffering or real danger. For how can we feel fear when we do not believe there to be any danger? How can we feel pity when we do not believe there to be any suffering? (Lamarque, 1981, p. 291)

The apparent tension between the beliefs we hold about the nature of fiction and the beliefs needed to explain our being moved by fictional characters and situations can, presumably, leave us with two broadly conceived options. The first is that we somehow look for alternative ways of construing the phenomenon of an emotional response to fiction which would depict such an emotion as *not* involving a set of inconsistent beliefs as delineated above. The second option is to concede that it is not possible to give a veridical description of fictional emotions that does not include reference to a set of inconsistent beliefs, which means admitting that fictional emotions exist as a rationally inexplicable category of mental phenomena. Adopting the first option would imply that fictional emotions do fall within the jurisdiction of mental phenomena that are amenable to rational explanation, just as real-life or 'factual' emotions are rationally explained. It would mean that these emotions do have a rational foundation provided either by some suitable belief or by some other mental state or attitude that acts as an effective substitute for belief. But if we resort to the second option, we shall have to concede that our emotional response to fiction is an irrational fact of our mental life, since it embodies incoherent attitudes on our part.

Most philosophers who have investigated the seemingly paradoxical nature of these mental states have opted for the first alternative.[1] This is understandable in view of the fact that there seems to be something counter-intuitive about relegating our affective reactions to works of fiction to the sphere of the irrational. Indeed, endorsing this thesis may have the undesirable consequence of questioning the very sanity of aesthetic experience or emotional appreciation of works of art. Nonetheless, the irrationality thesis has been trenchantly supported by one philosopher, Colin Radford (Radford, 1975, 1977, 1982a, 1982b), who claims to see no possibility of removing this paradox. It is his firm conviction that there is no rationally satisfactory answer to the following question: How can we feel genuinely and involuntarily sad, and weep, as we do, knowing as we do that no one has suffered and died? (Radford, 1975, p. 77) After canvassing various other solutions to the paradox, none of which he considers to be tenable, he advocates the acceptance of what he deems inevitable: 'I am left with the conclusion that our being moved in certain ways by works of art, though very 'natural' to us and in that way only too intelligible, involves us in inconsistency and so incoherence'. (p. 78) Radford draws analogical support for his claim by alluding to other alleged irrational phenomena 'in which

[1] Lamarque (1981), Mounce (1980), Novitz (1980), Price (1964), Schaper (1978), Skulsky (1980), Walton (1978), Weston 1975).

we are similarly inconsistent, *i.e.* in which, while knowing that
something is or is not so, we spontaneously behave, or even may
be unable to stop ourselves from behaving, as if we believed the
contrary'. (Ibid.) For example, a tennis player who sees his shot
going into the net often gives a little involuntary jump to lift the ball
over. Here, as Radford thinks, his behaviour is explicable, not as a
purely expressive jump, as some people might be inclined to think it
is, but as a jump which is (irrationally) believed to help lift the ball
over the net. Furthermore, Radford talks about our fear of death as
involving the belief that one's death is somehow dangerous or
harmful to one's life, while one also believes that there is literally
nothing to fear in that one does not participate in life when one is
dead.[2] Thus, surprising though it might appear to be, rational
human beings are not only capable of succumbing to irrationality,
they are easily prone to it.

2.2 THE ALLEGATION OF IRRATIONALITY *VIS-A-VIS* TWO SENSES OF RATIONALITY

Radford's analysis of emotions in terms of appropriate beliefs is
quite in conformity with our account presented in Chapter One. His
answer to the general question—'What is it to be moved by something's happening to someone?' (1975, p. 67)—is that 'I can only
be moved by someone's plight if I believe that something terrible
has happened to him'. (1975, p. 68) Why is this true about human
emotions? In order to demonstrate the necessity of belief for emotional
experience, he invites us to

suppose that you have a drink with a man who proceeds to tell you a harrowing
story about his sister and you are harrowed. After enjoying your reaction
he tells you that he doesn't have a sister, that he has invented the story.
[Here] we might say that the 'heroine' of the account is fictitious. [And]
once you have been told this you can no longer be harrowed. Indeed it is
possible that you may be embarrassed by your reaction precisely because it
so clearly indicates that you were taken in—and you may feel embarrassed
for the story-teller that he could have behaved in such a way. But the

---

[2]   Radford's two examples—the tennis player's jump and the fear of death—are both
weak in their own right. To take the first example first, if the tennis player's jump is
*in*voluntary, would it not be more appropriate to assess it as *non*-rational rather than
*ir*rational? And does the tennis player really *believe* that his jump will help lift the ball
over? About the second example, it can be said that many people do not want their
life to be terminated and hence fear death for that reason; not because of some possible
harm in this life or in an after-life. For an interesting discussion, see Rorty (1983).

possibility of your being harrowed again seems to require that you believe that someone suffered. (Ibid.)

What is described above is true of 'normal' emotional reactions and thus it sets the paradigm of the rationality of an emotional response to something, or the cessation of the emotion in accordance with the realization of the falsity of the belief essentially included in it. For if someone could not stop being harrowed even after being told that the story was a fiction, his emotional state would be of serious concern, not just as a matter of psychopathology but also as a problem requiring conceptual reconsideration. It would seem to present a case of cognitive dissonance. As such, it seems compelling to assert that the belief characteristic of an emotion is the reason why the subject has the emotion. To offer the fact that the subject has this belief is to provide a rational answer to the question of why he has the emotion.

In a subsequent article Radford reiterates that 'in order to feel concern for someone in a certain situation or to be moved by someone's plight, one has to believe that he is, or is more or less likely to be, in some parlous situation or desperate plight, and so, *a fortiori* that there is such a person'. (Radford, 1977, p. 208) However, continues Radford, the victim need not be perceived in his victimized condition; the mere thought of him being in that condition can also move us. 'But here thought implies belief. We have to believe in his torment to be tormented by it. When we say that the thought of his plight moves us to tears or grieves us, it is thinking of or contemplating suffering which we believe to be actual or likely that does it'. (1975, p. 68) In other words, only an *asserted* thought, or *assented* thought, can be effective in affecting us. In a paradigm case, then, the appropriate asserted thought, or belief, lays the foundation on which the structure of the affective experience is erected.

However, Radford clarifies his position by stating unequivocally that the appropriate belief is a necessary condition only of our being 'unpuzzlingly, rationally, or coherently' moved. (1977, p. 210) The motive behind this specification is clearly that of not ruling out the existence of emotional phenomena in the explanation of which no suitable belief seems to be included. Our being moved by fictions is not unpuzzling, rational or coherent in that, in so responding to them, we are behaving in a way that is contrary to the way in which our belief in the nature of the real or 'factual' warrants us to behave. We are reacting as though we have mistaken fictions for facts, but our reaction is not reconcilable with our knowledge that our attention is directed on to fictions. Nonetheless, that we often do react in this incoherent way is a brute fact of our life. Hence the existence of irrationality is also a brute fact of our life.

What seems to be implicit in the above argument from Radford is that one cannot provide a universally necessary condition for the occurrence of emotions *simpliciter*. For we are faced with two categories of emotions—real-life and fictional—such that what is a necessary condition of the occurrence of an instance of the former category is not necessary for an instance of the latter to occur. Thus, if the necessary condition of having an emotion of the former type is C, then the statement 'C is a necessary condition of an "unpuzzling, rational, or coherent" emotion' does not permit us the further generalization 'C is a necessary condition of an emotion *simpliciter*'. But it is precisely because people can have some emotions puzzling. As he writes: 'And the reason why their response is puzzling is that since they do not believe that anyone is suffering, or is likely to suffer, they do not believe in the existence or possible existence of the suffering which disturbs or moves them; and so it would appear that there is nothing for them to be moved by or concerned about when they are moved by fictional suffering.' (1977, p. 209) Such responses are problematic.

However, we may ask, quite legitimately, why he does not want to give up the claim that C is a necessary condition of any emotion whatsoever *if* he concedes that some emotions can be had without satisfying this condition. Why should not the case of fictional emotions be used to show that such a necessary condition does not exist? Radford does not want this consequence to follow from this position, since it would then imply that we have no coherent, rationally explicable concept of emotion. It would also mean that we have no unequivocal reason to cite in giving an answer to the question of why we feel a certain emotion. So the said necessary condition must exist in order, at least, to save the case of paradigm or real-life emotions from the charge of irrationality.

But now we seem to be facing a serious question. If fictional emotions occur without satisfying the condition that is held to be necessary for an emotion to be unpuzzling, rational or coherent, then it is implausible to ask the subject of such an emotion why he feels it, or what the reason is for his having this emotion. But this seems counter-intuitive. For it is not just plausible but even desirable to give reasons for feeling sad or affected in other ways in a fictional context, just as we give reasons for these feelings when they occur in real-life context. Moreover, as in the real-life case, reasons can be subjected to some sort of evaluation by reference to a certain view of human life. In other words, there are reasons for fictional emotions: fictional emotions can be evaluated as reasonable responses on our part to fictional characters.

Yet this raises the problem of how such emotions can be evaluated as reasonable *if* it is held that no rational explanation can be provided to account for their occurrence. It is in view of such a perplexing situation that, I think, it is incumbent on us to gain, at first, a more systematic understanding of the relationship between rationality and irrationality. A judicious assessment of the alleged irrationality of fictional emotions ought to be subsequent to such a systematic grasp of the notion of rationality.

The word 'rational' is not univocal. Broadly conceived, there are two distinct senses in which it is used. Rationality in one sense is *categorial* or *descriptive*; in the other it is *evaluative* or *normative*.[3] Thus, when Aristotle asserts that man is a rational animal, what he attributes to men is not evaluative but categorial rationality. In other words, what he means by the assertion is not that human beings are not irrational, or incapable of being irrational, but that they are not non-rational. For (presumably) they are, unlike other animals, able to engage in ratiocinative reasoning. Human beings are categorized or described as reason-exercising creatures on earth.

Evaluative rationality finds its application when a categorially rational act, attitude or some other (reason-involving) human intentional phenomenon is assessed in terms of some normative standard or canon of practical or theoretical reasoning. For example, when we talk about an intentional act being irrational because it is done for a bad reason, or when an intentional attitude is criticized as irrational because it embodies an ill-founded, unjustified belief, we are judging the act or attitude in terms of evaluative rationality. Here our evaluation presupposes that we already have certain paradigms of good reason or justified belief which determine our standards of value. But in order to evaluate something as either rational (reasonable or justified) or irrational (unreasonable or

---

[3] On this distinction and its elucidation, see de Sousa (1979), pp. 41–63; also reprinted in Rorty (ed.) (1980), pp. 127–52.

unjustified) we must at first recognize that it is within the sphere of the categorially rational: that is, it is a phenomenon of the kind which satisfies the conditions of being the proper object of rational evaluation. (We would not evaluate the rationality or irrationality of earthquakes, volcanoes, avalanches or diseases of the body.) Thus, two pairs of contraries can be deduced from the above analysis: (1) categorially rational *versus* the non-rational, and (2) evaluatively rational *versus* the irrational. The non-rational is outside the precinct of rationality altogether. So what remains is the categorially rational, which opens itself to be assessed either for its evaluative rationality or (evaluative) irrationality. Evidently, then, the irrational cannot but be categorially rational. As Ronald de Sousa puts it, '[a]ny intentional state amenable to criticism in terms of canons of rationality must be described by some true description that represents the state as rational'. (de Sousa, 1979, p. 43)

To say that intentional states or events are categorially rational is to imply that such states or events have the *structure* of minimal rationality; they fit into a basic rational pattern constituted of beliefs, desires and other intentional attitudes. (For brevity's sake, I shall henceforward call this feature S-rationality.) Let us explain this in the context of an intentional act. An action is an S-rational event in that its occurrence is explained, both rationally and causally, by reference to a suitable combination of belief and desire (cf. Davidson, 1963). For example, if I believe that I can save your life by taking you to the nearest infirmary, and I have the desire to save your life, then, *ceteris paribus*, I shall (normally) take you to the infirmary. Here my action will be said to be *rationalized* (in Davidson's sense) if it issues from this belief-desire pair. Thus, it is built into the concept of an intentional action that its structure is explicated in terms of a suitable combination of belief and desire. Or take the case of intention: someone intends to improve his married life by reading out the Bible to his newly wedded wife every Sunday afternoon. His intention must be explained by his desire to ameliorate their marriage and his belief that by reading out the Bible as a Sunday ritual the desired goal will be approximated. The intention is thus analysed as having its minimally rational structure provided by a suitable pair of belief and desire.

The existence of rational explanation of the above sort is a built-in aspect of intentional actions, intentions and other attitudes of mind. As Davidson says: 'Such explanations explain by rationalizing:

they enable us to see the events or attitudes as reasonable from a point of view of the agent. An aura of rationality, of fitting into a rational pattern, is thus inseparable from these phenomena, at least as long as they are described in psychological terms'. (Davidson, 1982, p. 289) So, in the case of emotions, a rational explanation of their occurrence is given in terms of the subject's belief about the object: reference to an appropriate belief is built into the concept of an emotion. The emotion is S-rationalized by the appropriate belief.

But an intentional state or event having the structure of rationality may turn out to be evaluatively irrational (alternatively it may be evaluatively rational), in that the constituent beliefs and desires or other attitudes may be erroneous, unjustified or overdetermined. (I shall call this feature E-rationality.) The combination of belief and desire adduced to explain the action or intention might not itself be E-rational. The agent might act on the basis of a belief which is not sufficiently warranted by evidence, or is superstitious. For instance, I might plan to buy an expensive car in the belief that I shall win the first prize on a particular week's Wintario draw, despite my awareness that the probability of my being the winner is ridiculously low. And I might desire to impregnate a woman notwithstanding my knowledge that I was impotent or she lacked fertility. Similarly, the intention of improving one's marriage by reciting the Bible on Sunday afternoons would be (evaluatively) irrational if the belief that it is possible to do so by engaging in this ritual is itself without any solid foundation, or is ill-founded (e.g. the next-door neighbour told the subject to do so). It may be said that such acts or intentions are deficient in the dimension of E-rationality. Nevertheless, both are S-rational in that a belief-desire combination is available to explain the structure of each.

An emotion is, analogously, E-rationally deficient (or irrational) if the constituent belief, required by its formal object, is ill-founded. My fear at the sudden announcement that the apparently unnumbered room in the hotel where I am staying for the night is actually room 13 would be deemed irrational if my belief that the number 13 is ominously unlucky is based on no reasonable evidence. Also, an emotion can be irrational even when the constituent belief is well-founded. This type of irrationality is ascribed to what is described as *inordinate* emotions, by which is meant that the degree of intensity and magnitude of the emotional reaction goes beyond the amount proportionate to the belief.[4] However, it would not be an irrational emotion in either case if it were not at first recognized as an *emotion*, that is, an affective experience founded on a suitable belief. For an emotion must be had before it can be evaluated as reasonable or unreasonable. Whether the constituent belief is unreasonable or not, the belief is essential to the identification and characterization of the emotion. Hence the emotion is S-rational even when it is not E-rational.

The upshot of the foregoing discussion is that irrationality occurs within the house of reason. Our emotions', being E-irrational is not only consistent with their being S-rational, but necessarily so. To be either E-rational or E-irrational is to be S-rational. Irrationality is reason or rationality gone awry.[5]

At this stage we can aptly return to Radford's allegation and

---

[4] Jerome Shaffer maintains that the irrationality of *inordinate* emotions is more of an exception than a rule and that we should not make too much of this exception. As he writes:

'It would be wrong to conclude that less than inordinate amounts of emotions are reasonable and their absence unreasonable, with the implication that the man who felt no fear in combat would be unreasonable. For it should be pointed out that what is not unreasonable is not necessarily reasonable, nor does it follow that failure to bet what I can afford to lose is unreasonable'. (Shaffer, 1983, pp. 164–5)

[5] As Davidson observes: 'When Hobbes says only man has "the privilege of absurdity" he suggests that only a rational creature can be irrational. Irrationality is a mental process or state—a rational process or state—gone wrong'. (Davidson, 1982, p. 289)

Moreover, the very recognition of some intentional state or event *as* irrational presupposes that it is possible to devise some rational conceptual scheme in terms of which their irrationality can be explained and understood. And such explanation or understanding will embody a reference to certain conditions, perhaps causal, which are adduced to account for their occurrence. Indeed, psychoanalytic theory as developed by Freud claims to provide a conceptual framework within which to describe and understand irrationality of various kinds, including the psychopathology of our everyday life. The existence of such theories implies that irrationality, even in its apparently paradoxical form, *can* be explained rationally. Even irrational mental events and states seem to be structured in certain ways. When rational integrity breaks down within our mind, we sink into irrationality, so to speak, in certain structured ways. In this connection it would be appropriate to highlight Jerome Neu's insightful remark:

Psychological problems are sometimes in some ways logical problems. Our lives do not simply fall apart, they collapse in structured ways, and the fault lines are marked by our concepts. Our ways of understanding and describing our psychological states often reveal (and sometimes limit) the potentials in those states themselves, the potentials both for development and for disorder. That this should be so may be explained through considering the roles of our concepts and beliefs in constituting our emotions and other mental states. (Neu, 1980, p. 426)

review it in the light of the above analysis of rationality. The question is: What light does the above elucidation throw on his charge of the irrationality of fictional emotions? One thing which is quite clear is that he is not concerned with E-rational considerations. It is no purpose of his to examine the reasonableness or unreasonableness of the constituent beliefs of such emotions, or the unreasonableness of the affective reactions involved in them. Rather, he is trying to draw our attention to a much more fundamental theoretical problem which we must confront if we are to probe the nature of these emotions. It is that the suitable belief on which an emotion of this kind is supposed to be founded is a belief which is impossible to form, thus leaving us with the enigma of the possibility of the impossible. And in such a state of affairs E-rational considerations cannot get off the ground, since there is no rational basis which can be the proper object of an evaluation of the emotion. Thus, though the fact is undeniably present before us, its presence is elusive in that it does not seem to be amenable to explanation by the basic principle in terms of which facts of this class (emotions) are explained or described.

Radford's charge must therefore be related to the question of the S-rationality of fictional emotions. They are within us as emotions notwithstanding the fact that there seems to be no S-rational structure to their constitution. But this creates a serious conceptual dilemma. On the one hand, we are compelled to categorize the given data as a phenomenon of emotion, and on the other we recognize that the phenomenon lacks the minimally rational structure to be described as an emotion. How can some mental state be described as an emotion if it does not conform to the structure which we have found to be essential to the existence of an emotion?

Radford's preferred way out of this dilemma is to admit that there are two classes of emotions, just as there are two classes of human behaviour in general: the class of coherent emotions and the class of incoherent, puzzling emotions. Irrational, incoherent, or puzzling emotions constitute a separate, fundamental category of its own, and they always defy S-rational classification or description. Indeed, he distinguishes between two senses of 'being moved' while discussing the *Sixth solution* to the puzzle: 'There is being moved (Sense 1) in real life and "being moved" (Sense 2) by what happens to fictional characters'. (Radford, 1975, p. 75) He thinks that 'being moved' (Sense 2) is an incoherent notion—meaning thereby that the minimal condition necessary for being moved (rationally) is not satisfied and yet one is actually (though irrationally) moved. But then he adds that there is also something common to being moved in either situation. 'And it is what is common to being moved in either situation which makes problematic one of the differences, *viz.*, the fact that belief is not necessary to the fictional situation'. (pp. 75–6) That is, granted that there are some differences between being moved by the death of a fictional character and being moved by the demise of, say, one's own father, the truth is still that 'such differences do not destroy the similarity of the response and *may even be said to require it.* . . . [And] the essential similarity seems to be that we are *saddened*'. (p. 77, both emphases are mine)

Now, to say that we are saddened or moved in both situations is not so much to specify what the common element between the two responses may be as merely to assert the fact. The specification must involve reference to the constitutive elements which are shared by both responses. It is true that, as emotional responses, part of the content of each is a certain kind of affective reaction or feeling—some sensational/physiological changes causing a particular type of behavioural manifestation in the subject. But the affective component, though essential to a state's being an emotion, is not in itself relevant to determining whether two distinct cases of mental states are emotions. Emotions are not classified by reference to the affective component. Rather, they are classified by reference to thoughts or beliefs involved in them. For emotions are intentional states or processes that admit of S-rational explanation, that is explanation in terms of beliefs and desires. Hence they fall under the category 'rational' as elucidated earlier. In contrast, the sensational/ physiological processes underlying emotion, taken by themselves, fall under the category 'non-rational'.

The similarity has therefore to be specified by reference to the thought, the cognitive-cum-evaluative core of the total mental state. namely the appropriate belief. It is only this aspect of the emotion which renders it an S-rational mental state or process. If this is true, then Radford has not succeeded in showing the essential similarity between the two emotional responses. The similarity cannot be shown, since fictional emotions are held to be lacking in the belief-component. And an emotion cannot be said to be similar to another emotion if the belief required by its formal object is absent in one of them. Strictly speaking, it is not at all clear why the one from which the appropriate belief is missing, or in which that belief cannot be involved, should be called an emotion. If it is not sufficient to identify or classify such a state of mind as an emotion merely by identifying its phenomenological similarity with a mental state that is an emotion proper, then Radford is not warranted in treating fictional emotions as emotions. Therefore it is puzzling once more as to why they are entitled to be *emotions* of the puzzling, incoherent and irrational category.

2.3 AN ALTERNATIVE APPROACH TO RESOLVE THE PARADOX AND RADFORD'S REJOINDER

The recalcitrant question underlying Radford's formulation of the nature of fictional emotion is: How is it that an affective response of this problematic kind can qualify as an emotion without fitting the basic S-rational pattern of an emotion? Perhaps the only way to avoid this quandary is to be able to show that some suitable belief does exist in the constitution of fictional emotions. But it is, at first sight, far from clear how such a solution can even be conceived. Nevertheless, two philosophers, in response to the alleged paradox, have recently explored a different direction. Michael Weston (Weston, 1975) and Peter Lamarque (Lamarque, 1981) find it necessary to change the direction of approach by shifting the focus of discussion away from belief on to the *object* of such emotions. They think that the key to a resolution of the alleged paradox lies in determining what exactly it is that fictional emotions are directed on to. In their observation Radford has failed to identify the real object and thereby misconstrued the intentionality of such mental states. In essence, they are intent on demonstrating the falsity of Radford's contention that there is, *in point of fact*, nothing to be moved *by*, or concerned *about*, when we watch a fictional performance.

Weston clearly states that the possibility of responding to the plight of a fictional character with a certain emotion does not depend on believing that someone is really a victim of such a plight. With reference to watching a performance of *Romeo and Juliet*, he writes: 'For me to feel saddened at Mercutio's death, I no more have to believe or half believe that someone is really dying on the stage than I have to believe or half believe that Renaissance Verona has been transported to the theatre in order to watch the play at all'. (p.84) So Radford does not, or should not, have a problem. However, it is not that belief is out of the question in this context. Rather, it is that the belief is not about someone really dying, or something actually happening to someone, in the fictional episode. In other words, the paradox of requiring the very belief which it is impossible to form does not arise *if* the proper object of such an emotion is identified and the required belief is related to it.

How is identification of the proper or real object possible? Weston's answer is that it is by recognizing a fictional character or episode *as part of a work of art* that the real object can be brought to light. The implication behind the underlined phrase is that if, for instance, Mercutio's death is recognized as an episode within the context of a work of art, that is as a fiction created by the artistic imagination, then it will be realized that what moves us is not the real death of anyone but the *idea* of such a case of death. Our being saddened by Mercutio's death is, in essence, our being saddened by the idea of such a death. Presumably Weston wants to argue that, while it is fictional that someone dies when Mercutio dies, there is nothing fictional about the idea of such a death—so long as the phenomenon of death is itself a fact of human reality, or human mortality. And the content of the idea is provided by our conception of life, our understanding of what it is for a particular life of a certain character to be tragically terminated by some unwholesome event. That Radford has a very narrow view about what sorts of things can move us is a belief which Weston expresses by arguing that

we can be moved, not merely by what has occurred or what is probable, but also by ideas. I can be saddened not only by the death of my child or the breakdown of your marriage, but also by the thought that even the most intimate and intense relationships must end. Such feelings are not responses to particular events but express, I think, a certain conception of life and are the product of reflection on it. (Weston, 1975, pp. 85–86)

In continuation of the elucidation of the point made above, he mentions the case of our being saddened or angered by reading accounts of war. When we are so saddened or angered, the object of our feeling is not the death and suffering of particular individuals, but the reflective, evaluative thought that some people can do terrible things to other people in pursuit of self-interest. Weston remarks: 'What I am responding to here is, we can say, a possibility of human life perceived through a certain conception of life'. (p. 86)

The above line of thinking is brought to bear on justifying the conclusion that, when we emotionally respond to works of fiction, our feeling is not directed on to an unreal person or fictitious event whom or which we know to be unreal, but to a certain idea about the plight of a person, or about some event of life, represented by the work. Such ideas grow out of a certain conception of life, in the light of which the depiction of the character or event is generally appreciated. Thus, the ordinary concept of emotional response to fictions has been reconstructed and reconstrued as our emotional response to ideas or thoughts about the vicissitudes of life illustrated through the sophisticated medium of artistic fictive representation. And these ideas or thoughts also provide the background and sense of works of art as a whole. It is, ultimately, such a life-conception by reference to which a rational explanation can be given of our affective responses to fictions. Weston elaborates this in the following words:

> It is never a misunderstanding [or inappropriate] to ask someone why he is moved by a particular fictional episode . . . The provision of such reasons is a description of the object of the observer's emotion. To be moved by Mercutio's death is to respond in the light of one's interpretation of that episode in the context of the play, and hence is part of one's response to the sense we see in the play as a whole. (p. 86)

Lamarque's account is, though different from Weston's in specific details, in general similar to the line of thinking which we have traced in the latter. He begins by addressing himself to the question: What are we responding *to* when we fear Othello and pity Desdemona? The answer is proposed in terms of how fictional characters 'enter' our world:

> What is it in our world that we respond to when we fear Othello and pity Desdemona? My suggestion is that fictional characters enter our world in the mundane guise of descriptions (or strictly the senses of descriptions) and become the objects of our emotional responses as mental representations or, as I shall call them, thought-contents characterized by those descriptions. Simply put, the fear and pity we feel for fictions are in fact directed at thoughts in our minds. (Lamarque, 1981, p. 293)

Here, again, the argument is basically that thoughts are the objects of fictional emotions. It is not fictional persons but thoughts about persons fictionally depicted by which we are moved. It may be wondered how the content of a fictional naming expression is no more than a complex of propositional thoughts. According to Lamarque, we do not conjure up a fictional being when we attend to a fictional character in a play or novel. Our affectively charged attentive process is not, in fact, a process that carries an imaginary person as the intentional object of our feelings. For this is not how the character enters into the mental process. In point of fact, 'when Desdemona enters our world she enters not as a person, not as an individual, not even as an imaginary being, but as a complex set of descriptions with their customary senses'. (p. 299)[6] That is to say, the name 'Desdemona' has only *internal reference* or reference *within a story*; from the external, real world point of view it does not refer to anyone. And from the latter standpoint we appreciate the fictional use of a name in terms of the suspension of the normal referential function of names. Fictional names do not actually refer to non-existent referents but only to their senses, and the senses are provided by descriptions in terms of which the characters are identified. Thus, 'Desdemona' represents the thought of a woman victimized in a certain way. Ultimately, therefore, the identity of Desdemona is characterized by reference to a complex set of descriptions available within the story: Desdemona amounts to a complex thought, and our so-called emotional response to 'her' is a response to this complex thought. And since thoughts are (psychologically) real, responding to them is not responding to anything fictional.

To substantiate the above thesis, Lamarque draws attention to the independence of thought and belief. How does his account avoid the paradox of belief? In his opinion, it is the fact that thought and belief are logically independent which absolves the issue of its apparent paradox. The point is argued for in the following passage:

The introduction of thought as the real object of our responses to fiction arises from our earlier paradox of belief. It is not meant as a general explanation of intentional objects. Suppose we claim to be frightened of Martians and Martians do not exist. If we believe that they exist then it is no help to introduce *thoughts* of Martians as an attempt to eliminate intentional objects. For the belief itself has already landed us with such objects. But if we do not believe

6   Lamarque is apprehensive of the controversial issue of whether names have sense or only reference. However, he finds it explanatorily helpful to appeal to the Fregean theory, which gives way to providing a more convenient theory of fictional names. The theory is, roughly, that the normal referential function of a name is suspended when it is used to 'designate' a fictional being. So what is left of the naming expression is its sense, and the sense is given by certain descriptions suitably derived from the fictional story. Thus, Lamarque suggests that we 'take the sense of a fictional name to be the "mode of presentation" of its referent within a story. That is, the sense of the name will be given by those descriptions used in the fiction, or derivable from the fiction, which characterize or identify its internal reference. The sense of the name "Desdemona", for example, is given by such descriptions as the following: the person who is named "Desdemona" in Shakespeare's play *Othello*, who loses her handkerchief, who talks innocently to Cassio, who is killed by her jealous husband, and so on. Only the sense of these descriptions survive in the real world, not its reference.' (p. 299)

that Martians exist but still claim to find them frightening then the introduction of thoughts as an intermediary has genuine explanatory value. We can be frightened by the thought of something without believing that there is anything real corresponding to the content of thought. (p. 294)

But why should the thought of Martians be frightening to us if we do not believe there are any Martians? This question may be raised by someone if the afore-stated distinction between belief and thought creates the impression that it embodies the claim that even the mere entertainment of thoughts (i.e. thoughts without beliefs) can move us, as though belief is not necessary for emotion. But Lamarque does not dismiss the role of belief in the analysis of fictional emotions. Instead he relates the required belief to the thought itself, not to the fictional character. He adds: 'At most we must simply believe that the thought is frightening. And that belief raises no paradox in relation to our other beliefs about fictions.' (Ibid.) This seems to yield the following analysis: I am frightened by the thought T because I believe that T is a frightening thought. Hence, being frightened at the thought T is (unlike being frightened by Othello) S-rational. (Whether it is also E-rational is a different question to be settled by evaluative or normative rather than structural criteria.)

It may be questioned whether the views of Lamarque and Weston are sufficiently alike so as to be non-misleadingly brought under one general approach. For one thing, while Weston postulates ideas as real objects of response by founding them in certain life-conceptions, Lamarque's semantic account incorporates no explicit reference to connecting his notion of thought (as the real object of response) with the general idea of a life-conception. Secondly, one may doubt if a semantic recasting of Weston's view—as the thesis that our emotional response to a fictional character is essentially a response to a complex of propositional thoughts—incurs no loss of meaning.

I believe that neither of these suspicions is true. With respect to the first, it can be replied that the idea of a life-conception is not only not out of place in Lamarque's overall account, but seems to be essentially implicit in it. For the thoughts by which we are moved when we attend, for example, to the unfolding of Desdemona's fate are evidently rooted in, and nourished by, a certain conception of life. The effectiveness of these thoughts so to move us is itself explicable in terms of such a life-conception. A particular conception of life constitutes the ideological matrix of such thoughts and provides them with the kind of legitimacy and appropriateness necessary to make them objects of our emotional responses.

Regarding the second point, it can be said that talk about a response to an idea embedded in a certain conception of life is another way of talking about a response to a complex propositional thought, in so far as the thought is placed within the context of a particular life. The object of response, the fictional character, is constituted of a complex set of propositions which has a complex sense in relation to a certain life-conception. And it is this sense towards which our response is directed.

It seems to me that a version of the Lamarque-Weston account contains an element of truth of some importance. What we gain from this account is the basis of a general evaluative belief that is necessary for the explanation of an emotion. It rightly indicates the vital role of an evaluative belief in the generation of an emotional response towards a fictional character, since it brings to the fore the notion of a complex thought about life that forms the basis of an evaluation of the character. Thus it is a significant advance in the direction of making clear how the depiction of a fictional life can be the object of our genuine emotional appreciation. Moreover, by postulating ideas, thoughts or senses as the real object of fictional emotions, this approach points to a way of avoiding the paradox of responding to something that is believed to be non-existent. Perhaps we could put this point by saying that the object of a fictional emotion has a psychological or 'ideological' reality, not existential reality in the robust realist's sense of the term 'existence'.

But to say that our response is directed towards the senses of thoughts or ideas about life is to imply that the object of a fictional emotion is always general. For example, when we respond to Anna Karenina with sadness, what we really respond to is not Anna but the general idea that it is very unfortunate and regrettable that a woman should be in such a miserable condition as described by Tolstoy. This interpretation does not allow the fictional character to be the focus of attention of our emotional state, that is, to be the intentional object of our response. It diffuses the so-called character into a set of ideas; the character is reduced to the illustration of the possibility of a certain kind of life. But this does not seem right. For when we respond to Anna Karenina we do not respond to women in general or women who have had, or could have, the kind of fate that Anna's life shows. We respond to a particular woman's fate—that woman whose life is so depicted in Tolstoy's *Anna Karenina*. The object of our response is individualized. Indeed, Radford himself emphasizes this while commenting on the *Fifth solution*, where he says that

we do not really weep for the pain that a real person might suffer, and which real persons have suffered, when we weep for Anna Karenina, even if we should not be moved by her story if it were not of that sort. We weep for *her*. We are moved by what happens to her, by the situation she gets into, and which is a pitiful one . . . (Radford, 1975, p. 75)

It is true that our sympathetic appreciation of the life of Anna Karenina involves understanding the implications of a certain kind of fate of life and the possibility of that fate befalling us. But this does not mean that our response to a work of fiction is simply a response to the sense of the work, or the idea which it generates. For to say this is to confuse the *object* of our response with what is actually the *basis* of the possibility of such a response. Radford's own rejoinder to this, directed against Weston, is that 'in reading the play [*Romeo and Juliet*] and seeing a performance, and responding to it, we respond imaginatively, not simply to the senses of the lines a spoken by a person . . . whom, however, we know to be fictional. And, I say, it is that fictional person who is the target of our tears when we are moved by his [Mercutio's] death'. (Radford, 1977, p. 212) To strengthen his argument, Radford could have added that it is *through* the senses of fictional sentences, ideas conveyed by means of other aesthetic mediums of fictional representations, that we respond to fictions. This would imply that understanding the senses or ideas is a *means* of response, not the object of response.

The above point can be expounded by reference to a real-life context. When we are moved in certain ways by reading about some event in a newspaper, our response is not so much to the senses of the sentences that we read as to the events or people delineated by the article. So the senses or ideas do not constitute the target but are, so to speak, part of the constitution of the intentional arrow which is aimed at some target.

When it comes to the question of an emotional reaction to a fictional object depicted in a film, the suggestion that one merely reacts to the thought of the object, rather than to the depiction of it, appears even less convincing. Here one's focus of attention seems to be on the image that appears on the screen, which means that the image of the fictional object has the best claim for being the object of the reaction. Radford's rejoinder to Lamarque is along this line of thought. Concerning fear evoked by horror films, he questions: 'Why is it false to say that it is because the moving picture of the slime looks so real and horrible that, when it suddenly appears, I involuntarily flinch, recoil, thrill in fear and horror?' (Radford, 1982a, p. 62) The question is intended as a rhetorical way of arguing that it is not the thought but the depicted scene of the slime which constitutes the real object of fear and horror. For, continues Radford, it is quite true that if the monster did not look real and horrible to the subject, but appeared stagy or silly (perhaps due to bad representation or performance), he would not flinch in fear but find it rather amusing and laugh.

What seems to be a fundamental disadvantage of the alternative account is that its main strategy, namely shifting the focus of inquiry from belief to object, has the consequence of providing an insufficient explanation of the problem. For the proffered explanation implicitly brings to the forefront what it is intended to put aside as unimportant, *viz.* the role of belief. Consider, at first, Lamarque's claim that thoughts can frighten us even though we do not believe there to be anything real corresponding to the content of such thoughts. Even if we concede that the object by which we are frightened is a thought, does this fact by itself suffice to give a rational account of our fear? Radford argues that it does not; and I think he rightly insists on the point that one must give a rational explanation of fear by reference to one's belief that the object is frightening. And this necessary condition is not satisfied by the mere existence of thoughts in our mind, whatever the thoughts might be about.

Radford tries to expound this point by reference to an example. Let us imagine that I am on my way home after seeing a monster film, and I walk along dark deserted streets. Having been made nervous by the horrifying scenes of the film, I am invaded by the thought of the monster and am frightened. Then it would be true to say that I am frightened by my thought; and it is commonplace for people to be thus frightened. Nevertheless, from the truth of this fact it cannot be concluded that my fear is rational, coherent or not absurd. The absurdity or incoherence lies in the fact that I am actually frightened by something despite my belief that it is not dangerous or harmful to me, that is, it is not something which can literally endanger my life. In other words, thoughts cannot hurt me, and yet I am frightened by them. Thoughts are not monsters in any straightforward way. So the paradox, or the crux of the problem, remains, and hence 'the fact that we are frightened by fictional thoughts does not solve the problem but forms part of it'. (Radford, 1982a, p. 62)

In reply to Weston's claim that our responses are not directed on to fictional persons and events (for we know that they are fictitious) but to a part of the *sense* of a work of fiction, Radford draws a crucial distinction which Weston fails to recognize. And failure to recognize this, he thinks, has led Weston to 'his consequent tendency to give a diminished account of the responses themselves.' (Radford, 1977, p. 211) He introduces the distinction in the following passage:

Thus there is a difference between understanding that the monster is a frightening *character*, i.e. a possibly hideous person in the novel or film who is dangerous to the other person in the novel or film, and being frightened by him *ourselves*. (And how can we be?) And there is a difference between understanding why Romeo is stricken by the death of Mercutio, and being moved to tears ourselves by the marvellous Mercutio's death. (pp. 211–12)

Suggested in the above passage is the point that there is no logical entailment between 'understanding that X is a frightening character' and 'being frightened by X ourselves'; the occurrence of the former is no guarantee of the occurrence of the latter. Presumably the implication is that understanding that the (fictional) monster is a frightening character, or understanding why Romeo is stricken by Mercutio's death, are, though constitutive of a necessary condition, not sufficient to make us feel fear at the thought of the monster, or feel sadness at the thought of Mercutio's death. Grasping the sense of a part of a work of art does not *eo ipso* elicit appropriate emotions towards that part. Radford, I think, wants to insist on the further condition that what is understood to be the case must also be believed actually to be the case. Only then will the emotion occur.

The conclusion of the discussion of this section is that the shift from belief to object is evasive. Reference to belief is necessary if our response to the object, howsoever it is construed, is to be rationally explained. However, we have noticed that the alternative account suggests well enough how fictional emotions involve evaluative beliefs of the appropriate sort. What it fails to provide is a proper substitute for the existential belief in the structure of a fictional emotion. Instead, by shifting the direction of approach from belief to object, it bypasses the issue.

2.4 RETROSPECT AND PROSPECT: FURTHER APPRAISALS

Although there is a grain of truth in the Lamarque-Weston proposal, it is not tenable in so far as if fails to secure the intentionality of fictional emotions. If thoughts or ideas are replaced as the real objects of fictional emotions, with the intention of rescuing them from irrationality, then it must be shown that the intentional link between them and thoughts or ideas is secured by suitable beliefs. That is to say, it must somehow be established that the thought in question must be believed to possess, or be invested with, that quality which is normally believed to be possessed by an object of a real-life emotion. The thought itself has to act as a proper substitute for the object and be apprehended as invested with the appropriate evoking property. But it is precisely this that we cannot, in any straightforward way, establish. For a thought about some fictional situation would have a content which is fictitious, a content not true of anything. Belief and fictional thought seem to form an inconsistent set, It is on account of this logical uncompromisability that, I think, Radfrod's steadfast adherence to the charge of irrationality has not been shaken by Lamarque and Weston.

Nevertheless, throwing fictional emotions outside the precinct of S-rationality is not only counter-intuitive but in conflict with the fact that we do extend S-rational concepts to apply within fictional contexts no less than within real-life contexts. In other words, we do use, and need to use, the language of belief, knowledge, truth and reason to consider why a certain affective reaction to a work of fiction manifests itself in the behaviour of the subject. Asked why I feel sad about Desdemona, I need to be able to answer by stating an appropriate belief about her fate. And sometimes it may even be apt to use E-rational concepts so as to say that it is *right* for me, or for you, to feel sad at her misfortune.[7] The possibility of such considerations presupposes that we are dealing with S-rational mental processes or states.

As H. O. Mounce has observed, since fictional emotions are as much a fact of our life as their 'factual' or real-life counterparts and yet they do not seem to accord with the principle of S-rationality, the problem is essentially one of a discrepancy or conflict between *facts* and *principle*. Mounce contends that Radford's argument is inspired by a slogan which professes an unacceptable ideology, and

---

[7] Conversely, someone might argue that it is *wrong* to feel that way. In either case we would then use E-rational language, that is the language of 'right' and 'wrong' which presupposes that the very subject under evaluation is S-rational.

the slogan is: 'where there is a discrepancy between one's principle and the facts, do not blame one's principle, blame the fact'. (Mounce, 1980, p. 186) The principle is that one cannot, for example, feel sadness unless one does believe that the object of one's sadness exists. The fact, which does not appear to be in conformity with the above principle, is that people do feel sad about fictional characters despite their knowledge of the fictionality of what they respond to. This fact 'contradicts' the principle. Faced with this unhappy situation, the question arises: Should we redescribe the facts so as somehow to conform to the principle, or should we leave the facts in their innocence and blame the principle itself?

Mounce's own answer is that we should blame the principle and replace it with another which is the true one.[8] But in my view the principle should not be blamed and abandoned altogether. For, in so far as real-life emotions are concerned, this principle is a verdict given by the tribunal of S-rationality, or the minimal rationality of paradigm emotions. And since the analysis of paradigm emotions must form the background of any analysis of fictional emotions, it is necessary that the principle remain as the focus of that background. The paradox arises because of the fact that statements about fictional emotions entail no existential commitment, whereas the principle requires that statements about emotions entail existential commitment if the emotions are to be rationally explainable mental occurrences. I suggest that we grant the *prima facie* plausibility of this paradox and work our way towards devising a principle that captures much of the spirit of the original principle without thereby involving existential commitment.

Something general needs to be said about the paradoxical nature of irrationality. The paradox of irrationality occurs when we encounter conceptual trouble in giving a coherent account of intentional states or processes in terms of S-rationality. A paradigm of such paradoxes is the case of *motivated* irrationality. (See Pears, 1982a & 1982b) Two typical examples are *akrasia* (weakness of the will, or not being in command of oneself) and self-deception. The akratic subject is one who, in spite of having reasons for judging a particular course of action best, yields to the temptation of doing something else intentionally and freely. Self-deception occurs when someone, in spite of having reasons for forming a particular belief, forms a

---

[8] Mounce's own proposed solution involves, not blaming the principle instead of facts, but giving a different principle, namely that 'Like objects evoke like reactions'. Mounce's proposal is criticized by Hanfling. (See Hanfling, 1983) See also Radford's rejoinder to Mounce in Radford (1982b).

different belief under the influence of a wish or desire. The paradoxes are, respectively, the following: How can anyone act against his own better judgement? How can anyone form a belief against the total weight of evidence available to himself? These paradoxes are deeply rooted in the nature of reasoning. They relate to the failure, within a single person, of coherence or consistency in the pattern of beliefs, attitudes, feelings, intentions and actions.

It should be remembered that the case of fictional emotions cannot be treated as one of *motivated* irrationality. We cannot examine the nature of the causation of a fictional emotion by reference to a wish or desire. For the alleged irrationality of fictional emotions is not motivated irrationality. Here the subject is not motivated by any wish or desire to experience an emotion that conflicts with the paradigm principle of explanation. He does not lack command over himself in that he is sufficiently cognizant of the fictionality of the object; nor is he influenced by a rebellious wish or desire to form a radically counter-evidential belief, namely that the object is real. So there is no *akrasia* in such emotions and they are not self-deceptive either. (If he is suffering from self-deception, then his case is different from that of a normal spectator or reader.)[9]

Therefore, what we must look for is a rational belief that is operative as a causative force underlying a fictional emotion. But since there does not seem to be any straightforward way of locating suitable beliefs in the constitution of such emotions, perhaps we ought to examine the nature of belief itself and attempt to bring out a belief *of a different order* which could be substituted for the *first-order* belief entailing existential commitment. If a new variant of belief, which does not entail existential commitment to the object, can be shown to be appropriate in relation to these emotions, then the principle of S-rationality can also be made more flexible in order to accommodate facts under question. It is to the exploration and amplification of such a possibility that the following chapter is devoted.

[9] H. H. Price considers whether our disbelief in the reality of the object is suspended, whether, that is, the subject achieves what Coleridge called 'willing suspension of disbelief'. But Price points out that the state of mind of the person watching a play or reading a novel is only 'in some ways' like that of one who believes; the likeness is never complete. (See Price, 1964)

Again, it is for the reasons given above (in the text) that it would be wrong to view the problem of emotional response to fiction as a species of self-deception. Therefore I disagree with Jerry L. Guthrie's contention that it is possible to propose a common solution to both the problems. (See Guthrie, 1981, pp. 65–75)

CHAPTER THREE

TWO REFORMIST THEORIES: SCHAPER AND WALTON

Our observations in Chapter Two have indicated that shifting the focus of discussion away from the question of belief, in relation to fictional emotions, to that of the objects of such emotions, does not so much help resolve the paradox as beg the very question. For if these emotions are said to be directed on to thoughts or ideas, as opposed to fictional persons and events, it must also be shown that the intentional link between the two is secured by suitable beliefs. But if it is known that the contents of such thoughts or ideas are fictitious—that is to say, it is known that they do not correspond to anything real—the required link cannot be established by belief. So we are back to the paradox.

Perhaps we have been forced to return to the paradox because we have adopted an overly simple view of the structure of our emotional response to fiction. The cognitive structure of such responses might actually be more complex than we have indicated thus far. Perhaps it is the failure to recognize this complexity that centrally leads Radford not only to discern a paradox, but to find such responses on the part of human beings inescapably paradoxical. Again, it might be the same failure that prevents Lamarque and Weston from developing an alternative theory that does not beg the question legitimately raised by Radford. Presumably they all have committed the common mistake of overlooking how sophisticated the structure of fictional emotion really is. To correct this mistake, perhaps we should examine more closely the beliefs which we hold about fictional characters and events, with a view to characterizing them in such a way that they will not be in conflict with our belief that we are not attending to anything real.

In this chapter I intend to discuss and criticize two variations of such an approach, propounded respectively by Eva Schaper (Schaper, 1978) and Kendall Walton (Walton, 1978a & 1978b). I shall call both theories instances of 'The Reformist Theory', since both Schaper and Walton explore the structure of fictional emotions and reform the notion of belief so as to establish that fictional emotions are caused by beliefs characterized in a special way.

3.1. THE ILLUSION OF A CONFLICT: SCHAPER'S DISCOVERY

Schaper formulates the paradox by introducing the following two philosophical principles (with the qualification that whatever dispute there may be about them is irrelevant to this discussion):[1]):

In the general context of belief and emotional response, two things seem uncontroversial: (A) knowing entails believing, and (B) an emotional response presupposes some beliefs (whether true or false) about that to which one responds. (Schaper, p. 31)

Given these principles, fictional emotions appear paradoxical. If we know, of some characters in fiction, that they do not have their counterparts in real life and that the events in which they are caught up never occurred, then it follows, from (A), that we believe there actually is nothing to respond to. Knowing that X is fictional entails believing that X does not exist and never existed. And if there is no belief that X is undergoing something, or something is happening to X due to certain circumstances, then from (B), indirectly, it follows that I cannot feel any emotion towards X. Directly it follows from (B) that I can feel a particular emotion towards X only if I believe that X is in some condition which has the quality or character suitably related to the emotion. For instance, if my emotion directed towards X is sorrow or sadness, then it implies that I believe X to be a victim of some misfortune. Conversely, if there is nothing for me to form the appropriate belief about—in case, that is, I believe X to be fictitious and hence do not believe X to have suffered any misfortune— then I cannot rationally feel sad towards X. But, paradoxically sometimes I *do* respond to a fictional X with sadness when X is presented to me in theatres, novels or paintings. So, apparently my emotional response to a fictional X violates principles (A) and (B). Emotional response to fiction seems to be in logical conflict with what we actually know and believe.

To avoid the conflict, Coleridge and others propose the theory that somehow our disbelief in fiction, which is a logical consequence of (A), has to be suspended. For only through such a suspension can the subject's mental attitude be transformed to yield to a frame of mind which can conform to the requirement specified by (B), if he is to be genuinely moved. But Schaper rightly questions exactly how the suspension of disbelief is supposed to work in the face of our explicit knowledge or belief that the object is unreal. How is it that

---

[1] Both H. A. Prichard and Zeno Vendler reject principle (A). See Prichard (1950), pp. 85–91 & 95–7 and Vendler (1972), Chapter V.

a work of fiction can make us willingly suspend our disbelief in the reality of what is presented?

In order to be clear about the above, Schaper suggests that we at first examine the notion of an ordinary suspension of belief or disbelief. Ordinarily, suspension of disbelief is accompanied by the corresponding suspension of the knowledge-claim about the object (or proposition about some state of affairs) disbelieved. For example, if yesterday I believed that there were a dozen eggs in the refrigerator and this belief was grounded in my knowing (remembering) that I had put twelve eggs in, the suspicion today that my unloyal wife might have given two eggs away to our next-door neighbour makes me not only suspend my belief but also my knowledge claim, until I have had a chance to check the refrigerator. Similarly, my disbelieving that there were fewer than twelve eggs in the refrigerator is suspended on the suspicion that my wife may have given away two of them: and my corresponding knowledge claim is also held in abeyance until I can confirm my suspicion.

But it seems that the suspension of disbelief in the sense explained above is not possible when we come to fictional characters and fictional events. For in this case suspending disbelief in fiction is not supposed to be accompanied by a corresponding suspension of the knowledge claim that what we are attending to is fictional. If a work of art is held to make us voluntarily suspend our disbelief in the reality of what is presented, and yet such disbelief is still entailed by our knowledge that we are dealing with persons and events that are not real, then, as Schaper points out, the following problem remains:

Only if I suspend the disbelief in their reality can I reasonably be moved by what happens, and only if I hold on to their non-reality can I avoid becoming the naive backwoodsman who jumps on to the stage trying to stop the characters in some Jacobean drama, say, from perpetrating their evil designs. (Schaper, p. 34)

Thus, if someone who feels fictional emotion is not to be construed as a naive backwoodsman, he must be held to hang on to the knowledge that he is dealing with fiction. But he cannot be regarded as knowing something which he does not believe, since that would violate principle (A). Therefore it seems that 'suspension of disbelief' can mean neither 'believing what he knows not to be the case' nor 'not believing what he knows to be the case'. In effect, the notion of the willing suspension of disbelief has no coherent application to the analysis of fictional emotions.

If our emotional response to fiction is not founded on the willing suspension of disbelief, could it be founded instead on what Henry H. Price called 'half-belief'? (Price, 1964, pp. 149–62) Price emphasizes that being in a state of half-belief does not consist in a person's believing something in a guarded or qualified fashion; rather, it is a matter of exhibiting strong signs of believing a given proposition in certain contexts and disbelieving it in other contexts. For example, a man is said to be a half-believer of the basic propositions of Theism if 'on some occasions he acts, feels and thinks (draws inferences) in much the same way as a person who does not believe these Theistic propositions [while] on other occasions he acts, feels and thinks in much the same way as a person who does not believe them, or even as a person would who had not heard of them at all'. (Price, p. 152) Other examples, indicated by Price, are superstitious beliefs, fantasies or delusions and some forms of aesthetic experience. Regarding the last example Price writes that

when [some people] become absorbed, as we say, in the novel or the play, the state they are in is not merely an absence of disbelief, but something more and something more positive. It is a state in which they almost believe (for the time being) that the events narrated by Sir Walter Scott did really happen as he describes them, or that Hamlet's father really was murdered by Hamlet's uncle. They do not quite believe it, but neither do they just refrain from disbelieving it. (Price, p. 155)

Schaper dismisses Price's theory on the ground that if the concept of half-belief is to provide an explanation of fictional emotions, then the explanation is given 'on the level of semi-delusion'. (Schaper, p. 36) For half-belief is a state of mind which resembles belief but is not full belief. She adds: 'Hence it is the more naive or less hardheaded readers and listeners who get "carried away" by fictional happenings into a state resembling belief—apparently half-believing that they are really happening here and now, for only in that way can the emotional response be explained.' (Schaper, pp. 36–7). Above all, Schaper is not convinced that the subject of a fictional emotion is in such a 'queer state'—a description given by Price himself—as half-belief.

Besides, if the subject actually were in a state of half-believing in (the reality of) fictions, then his mental state would be indistinguishable in psychological character from superstition and make-believe. For, as Schaper reports, in Price's account there is nothing to distinguish the psychological state of half-believing something in aesthetic contexts from the state of half-believing something which is said to occur in religious attitudes, superstitions or children's make-believe attitudes. She also thinks that analysing the nature of fictional emotions is by no means 'dealing with mild symptoms of mental derangement'. (Schaper, p. 37) In fact, she sees Price's discussion as merely taking us to the point where her own discussion began. As she writes:

Thus a man is said to be moved by a performance of *Hamlet*, and his emotions are said to be genuine and not just pretended emotions, but at the same time they are said to be 'not wholly serious'. But if we ask what *that* amounts to, the only answer apparently is that they are not wholly serious simply because they are responses to *fiction*. And that leaves everything as it was before. (Schaper, p. 37)

Getting back to where she started, Schaper wants to provide a new way of analysing the belief-structure underlying fictional emotions. She aims to show that, given this new analysis, our response to fiction not only occurs in conformity with principles (A) and (B), but its occurrence is necessarily occasioned by our beliefs about fiction which we form in accordance with principle (A). She thinks that, if the structure of such responses is examined with due consideration of their complexity, it becomes clear that the beliefs they presuppose are not in conflict with the beliefs which result from our knowing that we are dealing with fictions. She thinks that, on the contrary,

the beliefs which one holds about objects of our emotions in a play, a painting or a novel, and which are indeed presupposed by those emotions, are not only not in conflict with the beliefs we have about its being a novel or a play and so on that we are responding to, but can arise only because these latter beliefs are held in the first place. (Schaper, p. 38)

If Schaper is right, the alleged conflict between the belief that what we are attending to is fictional and the belief that some person is undergoing something in that fictional world is a result of misdescribing the complex structure of the concept of fiction as an object of our emotional appreciation. Indeed, it would follow that the beliefs about persons and events in a fictional world are not just compatible with the belief that they are all fictional; the former beliefs are made possible only if we have the latter beliefs. According to this account, my true belief that I am attending to a fictional work is what allows me to form those beliefs which are necessary to my being genuinely moved by the characters and the events in which they are caught up. In that case, what follows from (A) with regard to a fictional character or event forms the basis on which the beliefs required by (B) are generated and thereby some emotion is thereby evoked.

Let us call beliefs about fiction, the beliefs required by principle (A), A-beliefs, and beliefs necessarily involved in having an emotion, the beliefs required by principle (B), B-beliefs. Now let us examine more closely the relationship between A-beliefs and B-beliefs. It is not in spite of A-beliefs, but because of them, that our response can be properly and reasonably said to be directed towards, say, the unfolding of the fate of Desdemona, or the descent into the mine which occurs in Zola's *Germinal*. But what kind of belief is our B-belief about Desdemona's fate or the descent into the mine *in relation to* our A-belief that Desdemona is a fictional woman or the descent into the mine is a fictional event? And why is it still not true that our holding A-beliefs preclude the rational possibility of genuinely forming the relevant B-beliefs? Can the B-beliefs be treated as true beliefs once we adhere to the A-beliefs?

These questions about belief arise in the context of the general ontological distinction between reality and fiction. How can we preserve a unitary concept of belief when we simultaneously apply it to two ontologically different realms—the real and the fictional? How can I, for example, A-believe that there is no Prince of Denmark named 'Hamlet' in the real-world nation called 'Denmark' and, at the same time, B-believe that Hamlet loved Ophelia and hated his stepfather, etc.? One might well doubt whether I really believe anything when I say that I B-believe the something is the case in the face of A-believing that such a thing is not really the case. Perhaps we are bootlegging the concept of belief when we apply it indiscriminately to both fictional and factual contexts.

Schaper anticipates such questions by drawing a distinction between what she terms 'first-order' beliefs and 'second-order' beliefs. A first-order belief is a belief which is entailed by the believer's knowledge that he is dealing with fiction. For example, to know that one is watching a fictional performance of *Hamlet* is to have a first-order belief that there is no counterpart of the character Hamlet in the actual world and that an actual man, such as Sir Lawrence Olivier, is acting the role of the Prince of Denmark in accordance with the conventions of fictional performance. Above all, a first-order belief about fiction is grounded in a proper understanding of the concept of a work of fiction. In other words, first-order beliefs are beliefs *about* fiction.

On the other hand, a second-order belief is a belief about characters and events *in* fiction—those beliefs which are necessarily involved in our genuine emotional response to the occurrences of the fictional world. For example, my belief that Lady Macbeth is plotting a murder, that Anna Karenina is in mental anguish, or that Othello is overtaken by jealousy, are second-order beliefs about Lady Macbeth, Anna Karenina and Othello and what they do or feel. These beliefs are not just necessary for our being able to respond to these characters and events; they are also needed for the understanding and appreciation of the respective stories.

Having made the above distinction, Schaper now wants to demonstrate that first-order beliefs, or for my purpose A-beliefs, and second-order beliefs, or for my purpose B-beliefs, are not at variance with one another, since the two are not beliefs of the same order or standpoint. Thus, to B-believe that Hamlet loves Ophelia is not to believe anything that goes against A-believing that *Hamlet* is a work of fiction. She argues that only if the B-belief is taken to involve existential commitment to the actual existence of Hamlet and Ophelia can it conflict with the A-belief that *Hamlet* is a work of fiction and that the characters Hamlet and Ophelia are fictional. But, she continues, it is a salient feature of second-order beliefs that they do not entail existential commitment to what they are about. And in this respect such beliefs are not unique, since there are other sorts of beliefs that share the same feature. To this effect she offers the following argument:

The view that beliefs always involve commitment to the actual existence of that about which the belief is held conflicts not only with what we might feel we know about responding to fiction. It also conflicts in general with belief situations in which the issue of actual existence does not arise because the objects of such beliefs are, as the saying is, within somebody's intentionality. (Schaper, p. 41)

For example, she thinks that if Ralph believes that the next child he hopes for will develop the aptitude of playing the piano, he believes in something without believing in its actual existence. The object of his belief is in the realm of possibility.

Given the above analysis of a second-order belief, Schaper thinks that questions such as 'How can you genuinely feel sorry for Anna Karenina if you believe that she is only a fictional woman?' no longer appear baffling. For we are not in a situation whereby we assert, in B-believing that Anna Karenina is drifting closer and closer to disaster, that she actually lives somewhere in this world undergoing certain misfortune, in contradiction of our A-believing that she is no more than a product of Tolstoy's fictive imagination.

Accordingly, she holds that second-order beliefs lend themselves to truth-conditional assessment. She thinks that 'they are not in Russellian fashion all uniformly false' (p. 41), nor are they immune to being either true or false. In fact, these beliefs can be true in much the same way that beliefs which entail existential commitment can be true, provided we judge their truth or falsity by reference to what is actually stated in the 'text' of the work. As Schaper writes:

> Second-order beliefs, like first-order variety, are either true or false. Within the context of what we know to be a play, a novel, a painting and so on we have a perfectly serviceable analogue to the space-time coordinates which ordinarily allow for the determination of the truth-value of declarative sentences. In this obvious sense, second-order beliefs are true or false according to whether they are correctly or incorrectly identified within the analogue. (p. 40)

It is important for Schaper to emphasize that second-order beliefs about fictional personages are sometimes *true* beliefs as opposed to *illusory* beliefs. For an illusory belief will not be the proper foundation for a fictional emotion; nor will it be appropriate to an appreciation of a work of fiction. The subject of such an emotional appreciation is not in any kind of delusive or mistaken state of mind. But what exactly is it about first-order beliefs which accounts for the generation of second-order beliefs? In the absence of an explicit argument on this question in Schaper's own account, I want to suggest that the answer lies in the peculiarity and uniqueness of the aesthetic attitude. It seems plausible to postulate that her overall theory embraces a theory of the aesthetic attitude. This theory is (roughly) that our aesthetic appreciation of a work of fiction presupposes our having first-order beliefs about the work, *and* that our having these beliefs is accompanied by the simultaneous realization of the aesthetic significance of the work. This realization, in turn, at once elicits the relevant second-order beliefs about the happenings of a fictional world. In this regard the aesthetic attitude is contrasted with the 'natural', non-aesthetic attitude, which we adopt when, for example, we observe a painted canvas as merely a combination of certain pigmented patterns, not as an artistic representation of a rainbow or the sky. Similarly, we would be looking non-aesthetically at a piece of writing merely as a descriptive account of something and not as a play or novel or poem; and we would be listening to a symphony not as a symphony but merely as a certain combination of sound patterns. The distinguishing feature is that adopting the aesthetic attitude involves a departure from the natural attitude to a level of thinking whereby aesthetic, as opposed to natural, beliefs are rationally formed.

To put the above point somewhat differently, implicit in first-order beliefs about a work of fiction is an invitation to adopt the aesthetic attitude towards the work. Once this is understood, second-order beliefs about what is depicted or delineated in the work issue in the mode of appropriate appreciation of the work. Schaper also reiterates that it would be wrong to view second-order beliefs as ultimately reducible to first-order beliefs. For example, my beliefs about Othello's maddening jealousy, Desdemona's tragic end, or Herod's presiding over a massacre in Giotto's fresco of *The Slaughterhouse of the Innocents*, are not reducible to my beliefs about some fictional sentences and what they mean, or about a canvas or a wall with pigments on it. On the contrary, my proper appreciation of the given work of fiction requires that there be these two orders of beliefs. To quote Schaper: 'Beliefs about colour patches on a canvas or a wall, words on a page, musical notes in a score, actors on a stage, are what first makes possible my beliefs about Herod, Anna Karenina or Richard III, for example. But, to repeat, my beliefs about these personages are not beliefs about a canvas or wall, words on a page, or actors on a stage. They are beliefs about the doings and sufferings of these characters'. (Schaper, p. 41) And I think Schaper would say that those who find first-order beliefs and second-order beliefs mutually conflicting confuse the aesthetic attitude with the natural attitude. The illusion of a conflict arises only because the fictional object or event is assessed by denuding it of its aesthetic garb.

3.2 LACUNA AND INEFFICACY

It seems to me that there are mainly two difficulties in Schaper's theory: the first is a lacuna in her theory, and the second relates to the theory's explanatory inefficacy. Let us begin with the lacuna.

What is of cardinal importance to the viability of Schaper's theory is the provision of a complete explanation of the subject's transition from a mental state governed by a first-order belief to a state governed by second-order beliefs. It is quite plausible to accept her contention that appropriate emotional responses to fictions are not possible without recognizing that one is dealing with works of fiction and, thus, believing that the contents of second-order beliefs have no literal analogues in the actual world. Granted this, the problem is whether having A-beliefs in itself constitutes a sufficient explanation of the actual psychological transition to a state of mind whereby the subject forms appropriate B-beliefs.

I want to argue that A-believing that one is dealing with fictions is a necessary, but not a sufficient, condition of coming to B-believe, for example, that a character is going through the vicissitudes of his life in a fictional world. Being in a mental state conducive to the generation of B-beliefs is not a *direct* consequence of having A-beliefs, any more than being able to see things standing in front of oneself in broad daylight is a *direct* consequence of having one's eyes wide open (for the person might be blind). For the transition from the state of mind governed by A-beliefs to a state involving relevant B-beliefs is attitudinal. Therefore some condition over and above the acquisition of A-beliefs must be included to explain the attitudinal shift. To be precise, my argument is that Schaper has given only a *logical* condition of the possibility of the transition; but we also need a *psychological* condition by which to explain how, in effect, that possibility is actualized— that is to say, how the leap is actually taken from first-order beliefs to an attitude governed by second-order beliefs. But given Schaper's position, without the mediation of some psychological process or act or attitude, second-order beliefs would have to be spontaneously generated.

Furthermore, the existence or persistence of second-order beliefs presupposes the simultaneous maintenance of the aesthetic attiude. It is the aesthetic attitude which so to speak endows these beliefs with the reality or efficacy that they are alleged to have. Seen from the vantage point of the non-aesthetic, natural attitude, these beliefs are either false or irrational. So it would seem that the adoption of the aesthetic attitude necessitates that the natural attitude be, in some sense, put in abeyance. Now, if second-order beliefs are really effective in arousing emotions towards fictional objects and events, we do succeed in keeping the natural attitude away from interfering with our genuine psychological involvement with fictions. But the question then arises as to what exactly it is that explains our success in securing the aesthetic or second-order attitude. Is there not some specific mental act or attitude which lies behind this success? And is the aesthetic attitude itself not based on such a specific mental capacity?[2]

At this point I want to discuss the second difficulty, namely the explanatory inefficacy of Schaper's reformist theory. The problem in this case concerns the relationship between second-order beliefs and fictional emotions. In the preceding chapters we have discussed how the relationship between emotion and belief is both causal and rational. In keeping with this view, Schaper also wants to maintain that fictional emotions are rationally explained by reference to second-order beliefs, just as factual emotions are explained by reference to first-order beliefs. She thinks that it is rational for us to feel such emotions because we appropriately believe something or other about the characters for whom we have feeling. Let us assume for the moment that this account constitutes, *prima facie*, a satisfactory refutation of Radford's charge of irrationality.

Granted that second-order beliefs constitute reasons why fictional emotions are experienced, it must also be the case that they are causes of the occurrence of the emotions. For, in being a reason for the occurrence of an emotion, the appropriate belief must also play a causal role. But the question remains whether second-order beliefs, being what they are, can actually play a causal role in the generation of emotional experiences.

In order to answer the above question, it is necessary at first to determine precisely what the nature and status of second-order beliefs are as *beliefs*. To begin with, it is evident that these beliefs are only about what goes on in fictional worlds; otherwise they are, as Schaper herself admits, 'beliefs which are *as a matter of fact* false'. (p. 31, emphasis mine) Thus, the truth of these beliefs is specially secured—that is to say, they are true only in so far as they are about what happens in a fictional world. And it is not just that they are true because creators of works of fiction have invented certain characters

---

[2]In discussing and criticizing Schaper's theory, David Novitz addresses himself to this problem. His solution is that *imagination* is involved in our ability to make the required transition. As he writes: 'The problem, then, is to explain how the explicit knowledge which is required in order to understand that a work is fictional, can be rendered tacit so that we can properly understand the fiction. The solution can be found in an appeal to the imagination'. (Novitz, 1980, pp. 284–5)

It is also a central thesis of Roger Scruton that aesthetic experience, or our emotional response to fiction, is founded on imagination (Scruton, 1974). However, I postpone this discussion until the next chapter, where it figures as the main theme.

and described them as being caught up in certain events. Their truth also depends upon our *taking* the delineation as true to the fictionally projected world in question. This is so in that fictional beliefs and fictional truths are generated in part by our acceptance of the convention of fiction, which in turn occasions the shift of attitude from the natural to the aesthetic and enables us to view the projected world appropriately.

Thus it would be right to say that second-order beliefs are also specially secured or generated. But since their generation as well as persistence is founded on relevant first-order beliefs, second-order beliefs have a dependent, provisional or derivative status. And one important consequence of this is that they cease to be second-order beliefs or turn out to be false beliefs as soon as they are cut off from other beliefs on which they rest and by which they are bred.

How is it possible for second-order beliefs to exert the causal force required to elicit an emotion if they are no more than provisional assents to propositions about fictional phenomena? Being true only of fictional contexts, they are, strictly speaking, *counterfactual* beliefs, essentially contrasted with first-order, *factual* beliefs. However, they are not like other counterfactual beliefs which are attributed, for example, to dreamers who, in dreaming about something, form 'fictional' beliefs that they see something which is contrary to what the facts are during the period of their dreaming. Again, aesthetic counterfactual beliefs are also unlike fictional beliefs imputed to an insane person who imagines himself being someone else and thus believes himself to be the other person. In both the dream case and the case of pathological identification, the subjects hold fictional beliefs without being aware of the fictionality of their beliefs. The dreamer is lost in his dream world, and the insane person is entirely taken in by his compulsive fantasy.

The peculiarity of the two above-mentioned special cases is that here the beliefs, from the subjects' point of view, are not of a different order, elicited and sustained by some first-order beliefs. Rather, they are held by the subjects as first-order beliefs, much as people in normal circumstances hold factual beliefs. And it is precisely because these beliefs are deemed by the subjects to be factual beliefs that they are causally efficacious in bringing about emotional experiences. For it is part of the concept of a dream or madness of the extreme sort that the subject actually takes fictions for facts, which implies that his beliefs entail existential commitment.

The primary difference between aesthetic counterfactual beliefs and fictional beliefs involved in dreaming and psychosis, then, is that the distinction between fiction and reality does not collapse in the mind of the subject of the aesthetic case. In point of fact, the collapse of the distinction would mean, in Schaper's view, the impossibility of aesthetic appreciation. So, unlike the dreamer or the insane person, the subject of fictional emotions forms beliefs about objects and events in fiction while knowing that they are about fictions. In this sense second-order beliefs are *reflexive* beliefs. And the reflexive character of these beliefs is what, in part, accounts for the rationality of emotional responses to fictions.

The foregoing examination of the nature and status of aesthetic counterfactual beliefs seems to indicate that these beliefs cannot be causally potent on their own. They are causally efficacious only if their efficacy is derived from analogous first-order, factual beliefs. But how can any causative force be transferred to second-order beliefs when, following principle (A), they evolve and endure in the mind on the basis of, and in conjunction with, a first-order disbelief in propositions about their objects? How can second-order beliefs about fictional-world objects and events function in characteristically similar ways to factual beliefs about the happenings of the real world, if the former are formed knowingly and deliberately as *only* pertaining to fictions?

Thus, the conclusion seems to be forced on us that second-order beliefs are, in the ultimate analysis, tantamount to *putative* beliefs, stipulated by the convention of fiction. We are supposed to pretend to believe in some fictitious account, or what such an account depicts, much as we are supposed to pretend to believe in fictions in a game of make-believe. But here we are said not to be deceived by our own pretence, in the way children are taken in by their make-believe game. Yet we are also said to be moved by what we only putatively believe to be the case. The crux of the problem is how putative or pretended beliefs ever succeed in evoking emotions towards putative objects in the way genuine emotions are evoked towards objects that are believed to be actual or possible. For example, if I know or believe that there is no leopard in this room to frighten me and then pretend to believe that there is one just behind me, I cannot rationally feel fear as a result of what I believe. It follows from the very nature of pretence that my act of pretending to believe in the existence of a leopard would, so to speak, insulate my mental state from being affected by fear.[3]

---

[3] As Errol Bedford says, 'pretence is always insulated, as it were, from reality'. (Bedford, 1956–7, p. 284.)

If the above argument is right, then it follows that second-order beliefs are not causally efficacious in producing fictional emotions. And fictional emotions are, in Schaper's view, genuine emotional responses towards fictional characters and events. But if these beliefs are bereft of the causative force that is needed to move us genuinely, then they are in essence mere recognitions·on our part that, fictionally, something or other is the case. And mere recognition is not enough causally to explain why we feel any emotion towards fiction.

3.3. THE MAKE-BELIEVE THEORY: WALTON'S PROPOSAL

Walton propounds his version of the Reformist theory by retaining Schaper's principles (A) and (B). He agrees with her that the subject of a fictional emotion is fully aware of the fictionality of what he attends to. In other words, the subject holds first-order beliefs about fictions. Since he holds these beliefs, he is thereby led to engage in what Walton calls a 'game of make-believe' with fictionally depicted persons and events. While playing this game of make-believe, he forms what, following Ryle, might be called 'higher-order' beliefs which are appropriate to the understanding and appreciation of a given work of fiction or a fictional performance.[4] And when he experiences a certain emotion in response to what he watches or reads, his response is founded on, and explicable by reference to, make-believedly generated (higher-order) beliefs.

Walton illustrates his position by applying it to a case of fear felt towards a scene in a horror film. He calls the fear 'quasi-fear' so as to distinguish it from real life fear. He writes:

Here Charles's (actual) beliefs come into play. Charles believes (he knows) that make-believedly the green slime is bearing down on him and he is in danger of being destroyed by it. His quasi-fear results from this belief. What makes it make-believe that Charles is afraid rather than angry or excited or upset is the fact that his quasi-fear is caused by the belief that make-believedly he is in danger. (Walton, 1978a, p. 14)

However, the above passage concerns the subject's fear of something which he perceives as dangerous *to himself.* So, in order to include a similar point about sympathetic or empathetic fictional emotions, the following passage is relevant:

[4] Cf. 'The concept of make-believe is of a higher-order than that of belief.' Gilbert Ryle in Ryle (1949), p. 264.

We don't believe that there was a Huck Finn, but what interests us is the fact that *make-believedly* there was one, and that make-believedly he floated down the Mississippi and did various other things. (p. 23)

In the latter case as well, Walton says: '*Make-believedly* we do believe, we know, that Huck Finn floated down the Mississippi. And make-believedly we have various feelings and attitudes about him and his adventures'. (Ibid.)

Let us call Walton's two orders of belief 'belief' and 'make-belief' respectively. If the problem of the rationality of fictional emotions is to be solved in conformity with the requirements of Schaper's two principles, the following conditions must be satisfied: First, from (A), the possibility of fictional emotions must presuppose first-order beliefs entailed by the knowledge that one is dealing with fiction. Second, from (B), if fictional emotions are to be classified as rational responses, they must be shown to be founded on suitable beliefs— those beliefs by reference to which their occurrence can be rationally and causally explained. Since such beliefs cannot be first-order factual beliefs, Walton finds it necessary to introduce the concept of make-belief in order to fulfil the requirement specified by (B). Like Schaper, he also maintains that the belief that one is dealing with fictions becomes the occasion for adopting an attitude of a different order, whereby make-beliefs appropriate to the story are generated and emotional responses towards fictions are made possible. But, unlike Schaper, Walton construes these emotions as 'quasi-emotions' or make-believe emotions.

Presumably the qualification of fictional emotions as 'quasi-emotions' is intended as a way of distinguishing them from real-life or genuine emotions, such that emotions and quasi-emotions correspond to the parallel distinction drawn between belief and make-belief. It seems that all this is done in the belief that the quasi-ontological borderline between fiction and reality is to be recognized and the distinction taken seriously. According to Walton, there is a kind of asymmetry in the way real and fictional worlds are related. Obviously no *physical* action across these two worlds is possible in either direction. Within a particular fictional world Othello can kill Desdemona; within the real world, Lee Harvey Oswald can kill John F. Kennedy. But there is a logical barrier that prevents Oswald from killing Desdemona. Yet fictional worlds can *psychologically* act on real subjects, while we cannot act on fictional persons. And this action is asymmetrical. That is to say, we can be moved by characters in fictions but not conversely. The question then is whether this one-way psychological action between us in this world and fictional persons is to be construed as a cross-world action.

Walton contends that this action is not an occurrence across worlds but within a single world. Our being moved by characters in fiction is an event that takes place *in a fictional world*. What is implied by this is that our being moved by them is not a case of *really* being moved, but *fictionally* being moved. And that is why fictional emotions are characterized as quasi-emotions, founded on make-beliefs rather than on beliefs. To respond to a fictional character is to 'enter into' the fictional world in which the character lives, and to be part of that world make-believedly. In Walton's own words:

On my theory we accomplish the 'decrease of distance' (between the real and the fictional world) not by promoting fictions to our level but by descending to theirs. (More accurately, we *extend* ourselves to their level, since we do not stop actually existing when it becomes fictional that we exist.) (p. 23)

The above passage embodies a significant point for the development of Walton's theory. Cross-world psychological action is impossible if there is a logical barrier between fictional and real worlds. So our being emotionally affected by fictional characters must be a phenomenon of one and the same world. To say that this phenomenon occurs in the real world of ours would imply the implausible view that fictional beings actually exist. Therefore, the only alternative left for us is to say that real subjects like us must engage in some sort of imaginative fictionalization of our own existence so as to 'share' fictional worlds and respond psychologically to denizens of those worlds.

But does this not imply the equally implausible view that we somehow lose touch with reality and begin to live in a dream-like realm along with imaginary people? Walton wants to immunize his position from this objection by arguing that our imaginative descent into fictional worlds is quite compatible with our simultaneous existence in the actual world. He maintains that, as appreciators of fiction, we adopt a dual standpoint whereby we, as it were, see a fictional character both from inside the fictional world and from outside it at the same time. 'The reader is such that, fictionally, he knows that Tom of *The Adventures of Tom Sawyer* attended his own funeral, and he is such that fictionally he worries about Tom and Becky in the cave. At the same time the reader knows that no such persons as Tom and Becky ever existed'. (Walton, 1978b, p. 21) This dual standpoint adopted by appreciators is, in Walton's words, 'one of the most fundamental and important features of the human institution of fiction'. (pp. 21–2)

However, when we apprehend *from the outside* that Robinson Crusoe survived a shipwreck, or that Tom Sawyer was lost in the cave, we do not really believe in what we so apprehend in the way we believe, *from the inside*, that Robinson Crusoe or Tom Sawyer never existed, but only make-believe. Fictional assertions convey make-believedly generated truths and truths so generated are objects of make-beliefs, not of beliefs proper. Hence, when we feel relieved at Robinson Crusoe's surviving a shipwreck, or feel worried about Tom Sawyer's getting lost in the cave, our emotional responses to Robinson and Tom are not genuine responses but only quasi-emotional responses. So the correct construal of our being emotionally affected by fictional characters would be: 'make-believedly or fictionally we are moved', and not simply 'we are moved'. And from 'make-believedly we are moved' it does not follow that we are moved, but that we are, to use a peculiar phrase, quasi-moved. Thus, for Charles to be fictionally afraid is for Charles to be quasi-afraid. As Walton writes: 'What he actually experiences, his quasi-fear feelings, are not feelings of fear. But it is true *of them* that *make-believedly* they are feelings of fear'. (Walton, 1978a, p. 22)

Unlike Schaper, Walton is not vulnerable to the criticism that second-order beliefs cannot generate emotions, since for him the subject is not genuinely emotionally affected. But Walton still thinks that make-beliefs are causally efficacious in giving rise to distinctive psychological states which are quasi-emotional in character. The subject actually is in such a psychological state. 'And his being in this state', adds Walton,

is a result of awareness of certain make-believe truths: that make-believedly Willy [Willy Loman in Arthur Miller's *Death of a Salesman*] is an innocent victim of cruel circumstances, that make-believedly Tom and Becky might perish in the cave, and make-believedly Iago deceived Othello about Desdemona, that make-believedly Superman can do almost anything. The fact the person's psychological state is as it is, and is caused by such beliefs, makes it make-believe that he pities Willy, worries about Tom and Becky, hates Iago, or envies Superman. (Walton, 1978a, p. 21, emphasis mine)

What, on the whole, are the similarities and dissimilarities between the reformist proposals of Schaper and of Walton? The similarity consists in the fact that they both develop, and make use of, the concept of a second-order or higher-order belief. Like Schaper, Walton thinks that the subject believes, fictionally, that (for example)

Iago deceives Othello about Desdemona. But then Walton goes one significant step further to advocate not only that the subject's belief is fictional, but that it is also fictional that he hates Iago. Fictionality attaches itself both to the belief and to the affective experience resulting from this make-belief. And herein lies the difference between the two accounts. While beliefs can cause genuine emotions, make-beliefs are able to cause only fictional or make-believe emotions. Walton's proposal thus prescribes, not just a variation on the notion of emotion as well. But the latter variation is problematic, and it may be wondered whether this is introduced just to suit the purpose.

3.4. CRITICISM OF WALTON

In offering the make-believe theory of fictional emotions, Walton has advocated a conceptual reform to draw sharp categorial dichotomies, on the one hand between emotion and quasi-emotion, and on the other between belief and make-belief. The success or failure of this reformist proposal depends upon the plausibility or otherwise of these dichotomies. Is the concept of make-belief coherent as a *kind* of belief? Does the concept of quasi-emotions do justice to the actual nature of our emotional responses to fictions? In the following I shall be concerned with these two questions.

First, let us analyse in detail the concept of make-belief, or make-believedly generated belief, *vis-à-vis* belief proper. While properly to believe in something implies that one believes it to be (literally) true, *make*-believing in something implies that one believes it to be fictionally true. Make-beliefs thus generate fictional truths. A fictional truth is a fictional proposition which is true by reference to what is stated to be the case in the story in question. The central distinguishing feature in terms of which fictional truths are recognized as having a derivative or provisional status is that they are *generated* rather than directly registered. 'All fictional truths are in one way or another man-made', says Walton. (1978a, p. 10) They are recognized as truths only so long as the 'game of make-believe' is played; they are sustained by that game. And the fundamentally important point here is that the very act of engaging in a game of make-believe presupposes one's implicit or explicit acceptance of what is non-make-believedly or literally true, or of what one literally or non-make-believedly believes to be the case.

In playing a game of make-believe, one recognizes a principle which embodies the understanding or agreement that, if one believes that there is X (e.g. a glob of mud) but make-believes that it is Y (e.g. a mud pie), then it is fictional that there is Y. Walton formulates the principle as follows:

> Participants in a game of mud pies may decide to recognize a principle to the effect that whenever there is a glob of mud in a certain orange crate, it is 'true in the game of make-believe', i.e. it is fictional, that there is a pie in the oven. This fictional truth is a *make-believe* one. The principles in force in a game of make-believe are, of course, just those principles which participants in the game recognize or accept, or understand to be in force. (1978a, p. 11)

If the fact that the relevant principle is in force in a game of make-believe is always recognized, tacitly or explicitly, then every fictionally true proposition p generated by this game is understood to be 'grounded' in the non-fictional truth that it is *not really* the case that p. The prior acceptance of the non-fictional truth is what occasions, and makes possible, the actual engagement in the game, whereby p *emerges* as a true proposition. Thus, the truth as well as meaningfulness of p is, as it were, metaphysically anchored in the prior grasp of the truth that *in reality* it is not the case that p. Of course, this assumes our granting ontological priority to the reality of the actual world, which contains objects of our first-order, factual beliefs as well as the criterion of non-fictional, non-dependent truth or true propositions. But surely this is the minimal metaphysical presupposition necessary in order to have any theory of first-order belief and truth.

What follows from the foregoing analysis has an important bearing on the nature of make-belief in relation to its object. The differences between belief and make-belief consists precisely in the kind of attitude one has, in which one believes or make-believes something to be the case. For instance, there is an attitudinal difference between believing that X is a glob of mud and make-believing that it is a pie. Whereas the former consists in one's passive acceptance of the object in question as what it is really known to be, the latter involves one's actively adopting a higher-order stance of mind whereby one knowingly takes it as something that it is not.[5] Holding the belief that X is a glob of mud is to recognize the identity of X in a *categorical* frame of mind, whereas make-believing that X is a pie is to hold the thought

[5] Here I do not mean that perceptual recognition of objects is a passive affair. The use of the word 'passive' is intended merely to highlight the contrast between first-order perceptual belief and the relatively more 'active' higher-order act of make-belief.

of X's being a pie in a *hypothetical* frame of mind. But the hypothetical attitude of make-believing that X is a pie does not actually replace the categorical attitude of believing that X is in fact a glob of mud. On the contrary, the higher-order stance is founded on the first-order knowledge or belief about X. In other words, the categorical attitude underlies the hypothetical attitude.

Since the hypothetical attitude of make-believing in mud pies is essentially founded on the categorical attitude of believing that they are globs of mud, the subject will not be sincerely disposed to treat mud pies in the way he will be disposed to treat actual pies, namely to eat them himself or to give them to others to eat. From the rational standpoint, make-believers are not 'serious' about what they make-believe; otherwise they would end up believing in what is not the case. So they are as it were 'insincere' believers. But believing insincerely, in essence, amounts to pretending to believe, or to a pseudo-belief. For the sincerity condition is an essential feature of the phenomenology of belief as such—a feature which, in part, establishes the rational and causal linkage that exists between it and emotion. A rational emotion occurs precisely because the belief, on which it is founded, is a mode of authentically evaluating the nature of the object towards which the emotion is directed.

A make-belief is, by definition, insincerely accepting something to be the case, while sincerely believing that what is make-believed is actually not the case. In point of fact, it is because one can suspend the sincerity condition, required by the attitude of genuine belief, that one is able to engage in a game of make-believe. And that is why the attitude of make-belief is hypothetical. But an insincere, hypothetical attitude or mental state cannot be causally efficacious in disposing one to feel an emotion towards the object in the way a sincere, categorical attitude or state of mind can. For the hypothetical frame of mind is created by the withdrawal of the categorical attitude toward the object; and this withdrawal inhibits the issue of the disposition, which naturally attends the sincere, categorical attitude, to feel an emotion towards the object. As such, Walton can be accused of illegitimately investing make-beliefs with a causative force that they should not have.

In rebuttal of the above objection, Walton might agree that make-beliefs cannot be causally efficacious, but only in so far as the evocation of genuine emotional experience is concerned. He thinks that quasi-emotions are fictional, not genuine emotional experiences. In that case, perhaps, they can be caused by make-beliefs.

However, this response is founded on a fundamentally wrong assumption involved in Walton's overall theory. It is the view that fictional emotions stand to emotions as make-beliefs stand to beliefs—that is, the view that the former relationship parallels the latter. I think that beyond a certain point this parallel breaks down and in a very important sense fictional emotions *do not* stand to emotions as make-beliefs stand to beliefs. The parallel holds only to the extent that there are some significant differences between a particular fictional emotion and its real-life counterpart. For example, my actual encounter with King Kong would arouse a fear which is significantly different from the fear that I feel by facing a celluloid King Kong. In the former case my survival would very much be at stake.

The important sense in which the parallel does not hold relates to an analysis of the concept of a fictional emotion *vis-à-vis* the concept of make-belief. Whereas make-beliefs can be analysed against the background of first-order, factual beliefs and truth, and can thereby be reduced to pseudo-beliefs, fictional emotions cannot be similarly reduced to psychological states which are denied the status of genuine emotions. Whereas pretending to believe that I have won the Nobel peace prize occurs in a hypothetical attitude, adopted in full cognizance of the fact that I am not the winner, it makes no sense to talk about hypothetically feeling proud when I am not actually feeling proud. The categorical/hypothetical distinction cannot be applied to feelings or emotions. There cannot be a higher-order state of mind which counts as a make-believe pride.

I think that, contrary to Walton's contention, fictional emotions are not just a peculiar alternative to genuine emotions. They are themselves genuine emotions. To call them 'make-believe emotions' is therefore not to do justice to their actual nature. The crucial point is that an affective experience can be a genuine emotional experience without being a real-life emotion. Though fictionally generated, fictional emotions are *real* emotional experiences. But what reasons can be adduced in support of this claim?

Basically two reasons are available, and from two standpoints. Let me explain this by using Walton's example of Charles's fearing a fictional slimy monster. From the subjective, first-person standpoint, Charles's 'inner' experience is phenomenologically similar to the 'inner' state of someone who undergoes a real-life fear. Asked what it felt like watching the terrible green slime oozing slowly and relentlessly over the earth destroying everything in its path, Charles's natural response would be that he felt terrified. And it would be a first-person report of a genuine feeling of terror, though it is not a terror of life. So the question of what it is like to be in the state described above is answered, and can only be answered, in terms that are employed in describing an experience of fear or terror. And it is not just a contingent fact that Charles reports his own psychological state in these terms, nor is it a misuse of the term 'fear' or 'terror'. Indeed, any report given in terms other than fear would be a false characterization of Charles's mental state. In other words, his affective experience is necessarily identified by reference to fear. As Walton himself admits, 'he is in a state which is undeniably similar, in some respects, to that of a person who is frightened of a pending real-world disaster'. (1978a, p. 6) Hence to categorize his experience as 'quasi-fear' and not as 'real fear' is to overlook an important similarity between its felt quality and the felt quality of a real-life fear.

Facts or symptoms revealed from the objective, third-person point of view also favour the plausibility of the claim that Charles is genuinely afraid, though not to the extent of trying to leave the theatre or taking other precautionary measures. He manifests physiological and behavioural symptoms which are normally identified as symptoms of fear. 'He cringes in his seat as the slime oozes slowly.... Charles emits a shriek and clutches desperately at his chair'. (p. 5) Besides, his muscles are tensed, his pulse quickens, his adrenalin flows at an increased rate, and so on.[6]

Walton would try to defend himself against the above argument by reiterating that, since Charles does not believe he is in danger of

[6]Novitz provides a similar argument. He invites us to consider the following case (through which he intends to establish that fictional sadness, for example, is not make-believe sadness but genuine sadness):

Someone reads Maggie Tulliver's drowning and feels sad. Tears roll down his cheeks and are furtively wiped away, there is a lump in his throat, and his voice, in speaking, is choked, husky, and unsteady. Occasionally he wipes his nose which is ominously red. In such a case we have a host of public manifestations of sadness. There is both first-person and third-person evidence for maintaining that the reader is genuinely sad. (Novitz, 1980, p. 285)

Kenny expresses the same opinion in the following: 'The tears which we shed while watching films, the shudders which we give while reading horror stories are real tears and real shudders; but the surroundings are not those of real horror'. (Kenny, 1963, p. 49)

being attacked by the slimy monster, he is not in a state of fear, but of make-believe fear. As he writes: 'The fact that Charles is fully aware that the slime is fictional is, I think, good reason to deny that what he feels is fear'. (p. 6) The belief condition is thus cited to be a necessary condition for a mental state's being properly called 'fear'. Accordingly, Charles's mental perturbation is designated as a state of quasi-fear.

But Walton does not mean by the above that a quasi-fear is a special kind of fear:

I do not mean that there is a special kind of fear, make-believe fear, which Charles experiences. What he actually experiences, his quasi-fear feelings, are not feelings of fear. But it is true *of them* that *make-believedly* they are feelings of fear. They generate *de re* make-believe truths about themselves, and so belong to the fictional world just as Charles himself does. (p. 22)

Walton's insistence that one cannot be said to be afraid of something if one does not believe oneself to be endangered by it rightly specifies a necessary condition of fear *which occurs in a real life* setting. But it does not follow from this that a case of fear, which occurs in a fictional setting and which the subject describes in much the same way as he would describe a real life analogue, has to be disqualified from being a genuine fear. Granted, it might be plausible to describe a fictional fear as not being a 'full-blooded' fear, since experiencing such a fear does not activate the desire to engage in the kind of action, defensive or offensive, which the subject would engage in if he were to experience a real life fear. Yet his mental state is sufficiently similar to the state of a real life fear to count as a case of a genuine feeling of fear.

Furthermore, it is a serious confusion of facts to treat these feelings as belonging to the fictional world in the way that Charles himself is alleged to belong to it. Charles belongs to the fictional world by make-believing himself to be there; he *supposes* that he is living in that world and participating with the denizens of that world. Thus, if it is fictional that Charles is interacting with fictional denizens, he is not actually a denizen of that world, just as it follows from my dreaming that I was strangled by a psychopath that I was not actually a victim of this dreadful event. But if make-believedly Charles was frightened by a horrifying object of the fictional world, then he actually was frightened.

The point is that while make-believedly belonging to a fictional world does not generate the (literal) truth that one is a denizen of that world, make-believedly feeling fear in response to something of that world does generate the (literal) truth that one is afraid, though not afraid of anything real. While Charles thinks *as if* he is confronted by a slimy monster, it is not *as if* he feels frightened. One cannot entertain a frightening experience in a hypothetical frame of mind in the way one can entertain in imagination being in a place where some frightening objects reside.

The conclusion then is that fictional fear is genuine fear and make-beliefs are not causally efficacious in generating such an emotional experience. Thus it appears compelling to invoke an appropriate belief which is endowed with the causative force necessary to make the subject actually feel fear. But precisely how this can be done is yet unknown.

The upshot of the reformist theories is that they are designed to explore the notion of belief and extend it so as to create the allied notions of a second-order belief or a higher-order belief, by reference to which the occurrence of fictional emotions is to be explained rationally and causally. Both versions of it are imaginative attempts to provide a theory which would render fictional emotions free from the charge of irrationality posed by Radford. Yet in the end neither version is viable. The so-called second-order or higher-order beliefs are bereft of the feature which normally makes a belief genuine, namely the feature of sincerity. As a result, they are incapable of causing genuine emotions.

Now, our examinations in this chapter may suggest that a theory is tenable only if it somehow transcends the recalcitrant problem of belief and introduces a different psychological condition which would do the job in place of belief. It is to such a radical approach that we shall turn in the next chapter.

CHAPTER FOUR

THE RADICAL THEORY: ROGER SCRUTON

4.1. A RADICAL BREAKTHROUGH

If the genuineness of fictional emotions is ascertained and neither belief nor any variation of belief is found to be able to determine the problematic intentional link between fictional emotions and their objects, one might then harbour the impression that the intentionality of fictional emotions arises through some mental state other than belief, or some state which is deemed to be an extension of belief. Indeed, such an impression might very well be reinforced by the realization of the consequences of the reformist approach. We saw in the previous chapter that the reformist theories were unsuccessful in their attempt to explain the causation of fictional emotions by reference to make-beliefs or second-order beliefs, since these so-called belief states or attitudes lack the causative force needed to evoke emotional experiences. We found that Schaper's condition (B) can only be satisfied by a first-order belief. But a fictional context does not seem to allow the possibility of a first-order belief and this puts the problem at a standstill.

Perhaps the only way out of this deadlock is to delimit the scope of principle (B) in order to establish that not every type of emotion presupposes, or is founded on, a belief about its object. This is not to say that principle (B) should be abandoned. For the condition laid out under (B) is perfectly true of the paradigmatic cases of emotions, namely real-life emotions. But it indicates that emotions felt in response to fictions constitute an autonomous category; and it is part of their autonomy that their intentionality is secured in a radically different way. Some principle other than (B) needs to be formulated in order to account for their occurrence.

This line of thinking has been recently pioneered by Roger Scruton. (Scruton, 1974)[1] In this chapter I shall offer a critical exposition of Scruton's theory. I shall discuss his views under the title 'the Radical

---

[1] The overall theory is presented in Part II of *Art and Imagination*, but the specific points are encapsulated in Chapters Six, Seven, Eight and Nine. All page references in this chapter are to this work.

theory'. The radical character of his theory is borne out by the fact
that, rather than revising or extending the notion of belief so as to
devise something like a make-belief or a second-order belief, Scruton
introduces a wholly different concept in order to explain the occurrence of fictional emotions, namely the *imagination*. Fictional
emotions are said to be founded not on belief but on imagination;
and imagination is held to be 'essentially contrasted with belief'.
(p. 76).

With respect to the proposal put forward by Schaper and Walton,
Scruton would say that their 'extended' beliefs are really misguided
attempts to come to terms with imagination. On being presented
with a work of art that depicts something fictional, we do not form
any sort of belief or quasi-belief about the represented object when
we respond to it with a particular emotion. Indeed our belief that we
are dealing with a fictional object or event is a conclusive reason for
not adopting the attitude of belief or half-belief towards the depicted
object. But the attitude that we actually adopt towards the object,
when we respond to it emotionally, is that of entertaining without
belief the thought of it. And to have a thought about something
without thereby believing in the thing's existence is, in Scruton's
opinion, to imagine the thing. Thus the structure of our emotional
response to fictions is provided by the imagination: such responses
are so to speak sustained by the imagination. As Scruton remarks:
'My experience of a work of art involves a distinctive order of intentionality, derived from imagination and divorced from belief and
judgement'. (p. 77)

In Scruton's own terminology, our emotional responses towards
works of fiction are 'aesthetic' responses or 'aesthetic' emotions—a
term that he introduces in order to distinguish such emotions from
real-life emotions. His views on the nature of aesthetic emotions are
grounded in a theory of aesthetic experience. According to him,
aesthetic experience is founded on a specific kind of thought that
differentiates it from non-aesthetic, real-life experience. Whereas
judgements about real-life experiences are cognitive, as they involve
beliefs about the experiences in question, judgements about aesthetic
experiences are non-cognitive in that they are made on the basis of
imagination and not of belief.[2] Hence, emotions felt in undergoing
aesthetic experiences are founded on thoughts the core of which is

---

[2] Scruton offers the general theory that, since judgements about aesthetic experiences are non-cognitive, they cannot be explained in terms of the conditions for their
truth. Rather, they must be explained in terms of the conditions for their *acceptance*.
These 'acceptance conditions' can be understood only if we first know what is meant

non-cognitive. Aesthetic emotions are 'imagined' emotions.

Nevertheless, Scruton thinks that non-cognitively based aesthetic emotions are still intimately linked with the real-life or ordinary emotions which are founded on beliefs. For the two types of emotions are not just comparable to one another. The 'imagined' emotions are identified and made clear by reference to their real-life counterparts. Thus our response of sadness to a man whom we imagine to be in an unfortunate situation in not just comparable to our response to the actual spectacle of such a man. It is only by reference to the spectacle of real-life sadness that our response to the imagined counterparts can be recognized as a response of *sadness*.

Granted this essential intimacy between aesthetic emotions and real-life emotions, the need arises to examine closely the contrast between imagination and belief. Especially, one expects to know more about the nature of 'imaginative' thought which provides the basis for our emotional response to works of art. It raises the problem of 'imaginative experience' alleged to have no cognitive content and therefore requires us to bring to light the character of this experience by placing it against the background of ordinary, cognitively grounded experience. Such an investigation presumably would identify both the logically distinguishable features of the two experiences and the similarity between the two underlying thought-processes that accounts for the essential comparability of aesthetic emotions to their real-life counterparts. Above all, it is to Scruton's theory of imagination that we now must turn.

4.2. THINKING WITHOUT BELIEVING: A THEORY OF IMAGINATION

If the thesis that imagination is essentially contrasted with belief is to be established, the theory of imagination has to be developed by describing the structural features of belief which are necessarily absent from the structure of imagination. Scruton therefore starts off with the concept of belief, with the aim of drawing out those features which make it 'a mode of thought' contrastible with the other mode of thought called 'imagination'.

According to Scruton, the best way to analyse the concept of belief is to discuss it in relation to the idea of assertion in language.[3] In his words:

by aesthetic experience. This theory attempts to show how aesthetic experience can be regarded as autonomous, even though it is intimately connected with ordinary, real-life experience for its full description.

[3] This is so because several philosophers have convincingly argued that the

Sentences and their meanings seem to provide the only sure access to the concept of belief, and this argues a connection between belief and language of a remarkable kind. . . . No merely animal behaviour can express the essential definiteness that must be described in terms of the correspondence between belief and language. To have a belief . . a creature must display the ability to assent to a sentence, or to use a sentence as a premise in a theoretical or practical reasoning. (pp. 84–5)

While sentences are paradigmatically used to *say* something, the things said can be grouped under two categories. Some things are said in sentences that occur in the form of assertions; others are said in sentences that occur in the unasserted form. For example, when one says, 'Suppose that p', 'It is possible that p', 'p implies q', 'I wish it were p', or 'What if it were p?', p occurs unasserted in each case. The proposition p is merely entertained, or held before one's mind. 'Indeed', adds Scruton, 'much of our more complex thought-processes . . . are of this kind, and we know exactly what it is to say "p" unasserted'. (p. 88).

On the other hand, Scruton maintains that if one asserts the proposition p, one does more than merely hold the proposition in mind. One judges that p is the case. And it is necessary for judging that p is the case that one believes that p, where this belief may be described by reference to the inner act of assenting to the truth of the proposition, or sincerely accepting the proposition as true. As such, an asserted proposition is tantamount to a judgement. Scruton thus connects the linguistic notion of an assertion to the notion of a thought and uses the phrase 'asserted thought' to refer to judgemental thought, or thought involving belief. On the other hand, he uses 'unasserted thoughts' to refer to thoughts that are non-judgemental or devoid of belief.

In developing the idea of an unasserted thought Scruton draws upon Frege's theory of meaning *vis-à-vis* the distinction between asserted and unasserted occurrences of a sentence, as expounded in the classic article 'Sense and Reference'.[4] According to Frege, the meaning of a sentence is independent of its being either asserted or unasserted: that is to say, assertedness is not part of the meaning of a sentence. Every declarative sentence has an assertible content in

concept of belief can be explicated in terms of the concept of an utterance or assertion in language. See Aune (1967), pp. 213ff.; Geach (1957), Sections 22–3 and Davidson (1969).

[4] Gottlob Frege, 'Sense and Reference', in Geach & Black (1952).

common to its asserted or unasserted uses. And the content of a declarative sentence is a thought (*gedanke*), which remains attached to the sentence regardless of whether the sentence is used assertedly or unassertedly. In other words, there is a common assertible content—a thought—which is shared by the sentence in both its asserted and unasserted uses; and it is this common content which is held in mind when one 'entertains' the proposition p represented by the sentence. The meaning of 'p' does not change regardless of whether the sentence is used to assert that p or to make a suspended judgement that p. Indeed the argument form *modus ponens* provides a formal proof of this claim. In deducing q from '$(p \rightarrow q)$ & p' we see that the meaning of 'p' does not change even though it occurs unasserted in one premise and asserted in the second premise. Hence the thought that p in either case—that is, whether asserted or unasserted—is the same thought-content.

What distinguishes an unasserted thought from its asserted counterpart is the *attitude* that the thinker adopts towards its content. Scruton holds that to have an asserted thought is to give assent to what the thought is about, where assent means belief. On the other hand, to entertain an unasserted thought is to withhold the attitude or assent or belief towards the referent of the thought. Thus the differentiating feature of these two species of thought is attitudinal. Detached from the attitude, the respective thoughts are one and the same. With reference to this intentional isomorphism, Scruton contends that 'what is before one's mind in entertaining p is precisely what is believed in believing that p. Thus when we imagine something, or tell a story, while being indifferent to its truth, the content of our thought is the content of a belief; but the thought-process itself is independent of belief'.[5] (p. 89) And it is this independence of the

---

[5] Scruton is by no means alone in giving this interpretation of Frege's theory of assertion. The following passage by Michael Dummett expresses a view that is significantly similar to the above interpretation:

Judging is to grasping a thought as assertion is to the expression of a thought. Merely to have a thought—in the sense of grasping it and fixing one's attention on it—is different from judging *that* the thought is true—from what Frege calls 'advancing from the thought to its truth-value'. The difference is the same as that between expressing the thought, without intending it to be understood as claiming that it is true, and asserting it. (Dummett, 1973, pp. 298–9)

Dummett's interpretation draws out the logical link between assertion and truth in contrast with the corresponding logical relation between unassertedness (of a thought) and (its) indifference to truth. It also shows that an additional step is taken in advancing from the mental state of holding a thought unassertedly to the state of

thought-process from belief that allows us, in his opinion, to be able to engage in a mode of thinking called 'imagination'. Imagination, then, is a species of unasserted thought.

Part of the concept of believing that *p* is accepting that *p* is true. A belief-sentence is necessarily subject to truth-conditional assessment. Scruton thinks that believing that *p* is a mode of cognizing that the state of affairs represented by *p* is instantiated. That is, belief consists in a cognitive state or attitude of mind.[6] On the other hand, imagination is held to be a non-cognitive state of mind and is, thus, sharply contrasted with belief. The concept of imagining that *p* does not entail truth-directed considerations. For in imagining the state of affairs represented by *p* no claim is being made regarding the existence of the state of affairs. One's attention is simply fixed on the thought that *p*, which involves merely grasping the (sense of the) thought. And if the thought that *p* turns out to be true, it would not mean that that aforementioned entailment does not hold. For it is part of the concept of imagining-that-*p* that an imagination-sentence is not intended to be assessed in terms of assignment of truth-values.[7]

asserting it and thereby claiming it to be true. What consists in taking this additional step is the attitude of assent or belief.

John Searle has recently said the same thing concerning the contrast between imagination and belief. But, I think, he puts the point in a misleading way when he says that 'in imagination the agent has a series of representations, but the mind-to-world direction of fit is broken by the fact that the representative contents are not contents of beliefs but are simply entertained'. (Searle, 1983, p. 18) What is misleading about his remark is the denial that the representative contents of imagination are contents of belief. For the thought-content of imagination is also the content of a belief, except that the thought is unasserted.

[6] This point is more implicit than explicit. However, there is an explicit reference to it at the end of Chapter Six of *Art and Imagination*. Philosophical qualms about this view are very likely to arise. For the varieties of belief might not all be so easily slotted under the 'cognitive' rubric.

[7] Searle explains the nature of imagination in relation to the semantics of fictional discourse. His views are interestingly similar to Scruton's view that imagination is indifferent to truth. As Searle writes:

Fantasies and imaginings have contents and thus they are as if they had conditions of satisfaction, in the same way that a pretended (i.e. fictional) assertion has a content and therefore is as if it had truth conditions, but in both cases the commitments to the conditions of satisfaction are deliberately suspended. It is not a failure of a fictional assertion that it is not true and it is not a failure of a state of imagination that nothing in the world corresponds to it. (p. 18)

Searle's elaborate discussion of the problem of fiction is to be found in Searle, 1979, pp. 58–75.

A predecessor of the above view of fiction is J. O. Urmson. He maintains that

Scruton also distinguishes imagination from belief by arguing that the former goes beyond what is believed or strictly given. He wants to emphasize that one cannot be said to imagine X, or what it would be like if p, if the description given by him is already known to him, such that the description is tantamount to a definite assertion of how the things represented by X or p are. 'Thus', writes Scruton,

a man is not said to be imagining X (or what it would be like if p), if he produces his account on the basis of what he already knows—say, because X is before him and he is studying it, because p is true and he is observing the consequences of its truth; because he has been told, or remembers, the account he produces, because he has evidence, which in conjunction with knowledge that he already has, will enable him to deduce or predict his account of X or p. In other words, imagination goes beyond what is given in ordinary prediction and belief'. (pp. 97–8)

Thus, although the content of the thought involved in imagining X is one and the same as the content of the thought underlying the belief in X, the imaginative stance with regard to X is essentially contrasted with the stance of belief taken towards X. While the believer is committed to the actuality of X, the imaginer is not. In Scruton's characterization, 'the mental life of the imagination [is] quite different from that of belief'. (p. 128)

4.3. 'IMAGINED FEELINGS': A THEORY OF AESTHETIC EMOTION

If the intentionality of aesthetic emotions is to be secured not by belief but by imagination, it is necessary to consider how emotions of this kind stand in relation to emotions that are founded on, and grow out of, belief. More importantly, attention needs to be focused on the problem of the *expression* of aesthetic emotions *vis-à-vis* the expression of real-life emotions. For it is not just conceivable but quite reasonable to think that an emotion which is not backed up by

making up fiction is not a case of stating, or asserting, or propounding a proposition and includes no acts such as referring. Fiction has the external form of history and biography, but is neither. . . . It is as possible to go through the motions of writing history or biography without actually doing so as it is possible to go through the motions of playing chess without actually doing so. In the case of fiction 'Is it true?' will be inappropriate for the same reason as 'Who won?' is inappropriate to the mock-chess. (Urmson, 1976, pp. 155–6)

Urmson also refers to Hume's remark that poets are liars and interprets this remark as tantamount to the view that what is fictional is false. Perhaps Urmson would say that Hume's view rests on a category mistake.

belief will find its public manifestation in characteristically different ways, in some respects, than the manner in which an emotion based on belief finds its typical expression. But it is also equally important to maintain that there is an essential continuity between real-life emotions and aesthetic emotions, and at the same time 'grant to these [aesthetic] emotions a measure of autonomy that has often been claimed for them'. (Scruton, p. 128)

In what relation does a particular work of art stand to a particular aesthetic (emotional) response where the response is directed towards that which is represented in the work? Scruton admits that this relation is intentional in that the response is founded on a certain conception of its object. 'We might say', adds Scruton, 'without too much distortion of current usage, that this conception defines the "intentional object" of the responses'. (p. 74) But he argues that the intentionality of aesthetic emotions does not arise from belief. For one does not believe that there actually is an object instantiating the formal object of one's response. Instead, their intentionality arises through imagination. The depicted object or scene is conceived without belief, and some feeling is aroused as a result of thinking in this way. Thus, when a person views a painting that depicts a poor-looking waif, he imagines being a witness of an actual scene—the scene of a poor-looking waif. And if he feels sad or tender in response to what he 'imaginatively' sees, his feeling of sadness or tenderness is grounded in a thought-process that is not governed by belief, but by imagination.

However, the fictional scene whose reality or actuality is entertained in imagination stands to the aesthetic response in much the same way as a corresponding actual scene would stand to a corresponding 'real' response. In either case one uses the same emotion-term to describe both one's response to the scene and the scene itself. As Scruton says:

when I find a work of art sad, or see it as sad, I am responding to it in some way like the way I respond (under certain specifiable conditions) to sadness (to the sadness of a human being). It is because I respond to each in a similar way that I use the same term of each, and this response is the condition for the acceptance of the aesthetic description. (p. 72)

Hence, despite their intentionality being quite different from real-life emotions, aesthetic emotions stand to works of art in the emotion-object relationship. For in responding to what the work represents, an aesthetic emotion stands to the depicted object in much the same way as a real-life emotion stands to its object. And it is this similarity in what might be termed the 'pattern' of intentionality that accounts for the legitimate use of the same emotion-terms in either context. Scruton adds:

I use the term 'sad' spontaneously to describe all those objects that elicit in me responses analogous to my response to human sadness, and it is this that explains why I do not have to learn any new meaning for the term 'sad' in order to be disposed to use it, and understand it, in this extended sense. In other words, to find a work of art sad is to respond to it in the way I respond to a man when I am 'touched' by his sadness. (p. 72)

If the 'pattern' of aesthetic response is irreducibly analogous to that of emotional responses to real-life situations, then the recognition of a particular work of art must be parasitic upon the recognition of that emotion in an analogous real life situation. 'But', questions Scruton, 'how do we give content to this extremely simple theory that to see a work of art as sad is to respond to it in the way one responds to a man when touched by his sadness?' (p. 74) In fact he discerns a dilemma underlying this question, and expresses it in the following passage:

Let us call my response to human sadness R. Then plainly R is founded on, and grows out of, the belief that its object is sad. Now either this belief is to be considered as partly definitive of R (so that sadness is the formal object of R), or it is not. If it is considered as definitive of R then it must recur whenever R recurs—in particular it must recur when the object of R is not a man but, say, a work of art. From which it would follow that a work of art can be thought to be sad in exactly the same way that a man is thought to be sad, so that the 'recognition of sadness' in aesthetic experience is a matter of belief, and sadness is a common quality with which we are already familiar. If, on the other hand, the belief is not considered as partly definitive of R— if R can recur without it—then in what sense is it an important fact about R that it is directed towards human sadness, and by what right do we call its recurrence, in another context, the recognition of the sadness of the object? (pp. 75–6)

In other words, the dilemma arises from the fact that aesthetic sadness is presumed to be genuine sadness in spite of the absence of any belief regarding the existence of a sad situation. Why is it that the sadness, which is defined in real-life contexts by reference to an appropriate belief about the sad object, recurs in a context that excludes the rational possibility of forming the appropriate belief? It seems then that either aesthetic sadness has to be described as a kind of quasi-sadness, not genuine sadness, or the general thesis that emotions are defined by their appropriate beliefs has to be challenged.

Scruton's way out of this dilemma is to deny the thesis that the intentionality of emotions arises only through belief. He maintains that while, paradigmatically, the emotion-object relationship is secured by belief, it may equally be secured by imaginatively entertained, or unasserted, thought. Thus aesthetic emotions are genuine emotions elicited by imagination. However, the above is not a complete explanation of the situation. For, granted that aesthetic emotions are not quasi-emotions but irreducibly analogous to real life emotions, how can this be when the two cases of emotion are founded on essentially different thoughts, namely unasserted thought and belief? As Scruton himself asks: 'How, then, can the emotions be comparable, and how can one be used to identify and make clear the nature of the other?' (p. 128) Is the theory of imagination elucidated above in danger of destroying the essential continuity between aesthetic and non-aesthetic (real-life) emotions?

According to Scruton, the force of this difficulty is appreciated by realizing the intimacy of the connection between emotion and belief on the one hand, and emotion and desire on the other. If I am, for example, afraid of something then it follows that I believe that there is or might be something dangerous or harmful or disagreeable to me. It also follows that I desire to avoid the harmful or dangerous or disagreeable object. And without the belief characteristic of the emotion—in this case fear—I do not have the desire to avoid the object. Thus it may be said that 'an emotion is, normally, a complex of belief and desire, united in a causal relation'. (p. 128) But aesthetic fear is not founded on the belief that something (namely, the object represented in a work of art) is dangerous or harmful or disagreeable; hence it does not give rise to any desire to avoid the object. But this implies that aesthetic fear is not a complex of belief and desire at all. The question therefore arises as to how, or in what way, I may be said to feel anything resembling fear—when I do feel aesthetic fear—if neither the belief nor the desire characteristic of fear is involved in the constitution of my aesthetic response.[8] Is Scruton's aesthetic fear then reducible to Walton's quasi-fear?

[8] Since the difference in thought-process underlying aesthetic and real-life emotions implies a difference of identity of the two cases, and the identification requires that there be public expressions of both, Scruton opens up the issue in the following way: 'We must, then, try to show how someone manifests aesthetic emotion, and the expression of aesthetic emotion bears on its description. But if there are no beliefs on

Furthermore, the above question brings another problem in its train, namely the problem of the expression of aesthetic emotions. Normally it is the belief-desire complex underlying an emotion that occasions the emotion publicly to manifest itself in a certain way. And this complex plays a causal role in bringing about the characteristic expressions of emotions. But in the absence of any belief and any desire it is not at all clear how aesthetic emotions can find their expression. And since such emotions are said to be founded on unasserted thoughts, one might therefore wonder whether there is anything more to aesthetic experience than a thought. But in order to be a genuine *emotion*, there must be some affective content to aesthetic responses. And that affective aspect must find some sort of expression if a third-person identification of aesthetic emotions is to be possible.[9]

Scruton, however, tries to give answers to both these questions. With respect to the question of whether the expression of aesthetic experience is the expression of anything more than an unasserted thought, he answers that there *is* an affective content to the total expression of aesthetic experience.[10] If, on watching the scene of a waif in a work of art, a person remarks that the scene evokes a feeling of tenderness, or some such emotion, this remark must not be dismissed as metaphorical. The person might literally be moved by what he 'imaginatively' perceives. Of course, argues Scruton, the criterion for whether the person actually feels tenderness towards the depicted waif is not so much his behaviour as the description that he gives of his experience. And two reasons are adduced by him as to why the description *can* be taken as a criterion. The first is that the fact that the person wishes to describe his feelings in this way is something which should be taken seriously. For 'it is an integral part of the experience that *tenderness* should be called to mind'. (Scruton, p. 131) Secondly, the description that the person gives of the object of his feeling is couched in terms which can themselves be construed as an expression of feeling rather than merely an expression of thought. 'It is significant', writes Scruton, 'that he describes the painting in a certain tone of voice (not any tone of voice is appropriate to his remark), and that he makes connections with his attitudes and

which such emotions are founded, and no desires embodies in them, how are they expressed at all?.... Is the expression of aesthetic experience the expression of anything more than a thought?' (Scruton, p. 130)

[9] Scruton's argument for this claim is to be found in Scruton, pp. 130–1.

[10] See Scruton, p. 129ff.

emotions in other circumstances that are important to him'. (p. 131)

But how are we to judge that the person's remark about the work of art—that it evokes certain feelings in him—is not insincere? Scruton contends that we have a clear test of the sincerity of the person's remark in his subsequent behaviour in non-aesthetic, real life contexts.[11] That is to say, the sincerity of an emotional response to a work of art can be tested against the person's future behaviour and responses with regard to analogous real-life situations. For example, a person who declares that his tender feelings have been awakened by the scene of a depicted waif is at variance with himself when he fails to feel tenderness towards an actual waif. From this Scruton wants to conclude that there is a necessary link between imagination-based emotions and the appropriate dispositions and behavioural manifestations that are typically expressive of belief-based emotions. The following passage encapsulates this conclusion:

There is a non-contingent connnection, therefore, between imagined emotions and the behaviour that, in other circumstances, counts as an expression of the corresponding 'real' emotion. What I feel in the presence of works of art may find its ultimate expression in my behaviour towards my fellows. My 'imagined' feelings can show their effects in the expression of their 'real' counterparts. (p. 131)

However, even if the possibility of testing the sincerity of the person's remark supports the claim that there is an affective content to aesthetic experience over and above the cognitive content provided by an unasserted thought, what is yet to be brought to light is exactly how an aesthetic emotion finds its expression through sheer imagination. This is the first question mentioned earlier, and it is also the more important one for Scruton's purpose. For what still remains in the dark is how a mental state founded on an unasserted thought embodies an affective element, and what causes that affective reaction to occur.

Let us consider the case of our feeling sad at the plight of Anna Karenina. The thought is simply entertained that Anna is in circumstances which make her life drift closer and closer to a disaster. When we entertain this unasserted thought, we do not, according to Scruton's analysis, come to have a desire to do something for Anna—

---

[11] Concerning this argument, Stephen Davies's comment on Scruton is worth quoting. Davies remarks that 'it should be noted that *usually* to describe a response to a work of art as insincere is to claim that the response is non-aesthetic. We do not, as Scruton implies, accept the possibility of insincere, aesthetically proper responses.' (Davies, 1983, p. 47, fn. 9)

the desire which we would normally have if we were to think of a real woman suffering from a similar plight. This follows from Scruton's condition that without the relevant belief the desire appropriate to the belief cannot arise. And yet it is only the presence of some such felt desire, or some simulacrum thereof, which can provide an affective content to my otherwise purely cognitive mental state. The fact that we *feel* sad has to be explained by reference to the element of desire. There must be some imagined analogue of desire parallel to the way there is an unasserted thought as an imagined analogue of belief. Is it then an 'unasserted desire' which accounts for our feeling sadness towards Anna Karenina?

Scruton seems to feel somewhat strained in attempting to meet the last condition. But he also has to explicate the apparently baffling notion which I have called 'unasserted desire'. Now, he thinks that just as one can entertain thoughts unasserted, so one can also entertain desires that would, in normal circumstances, arise from these thoughts (that is, when these thoughts are tantamount to beliefs). 'In other words', continues Scruton, 'just as I may recreate in my imagination the thoughts that I would have, so can I recreate the feelings to which these thoughts give rise'. (p. 129) In describing the emotion that a person feels towards a fictionally depicted woman, therefore, we refer to the 'imagined counterpart' of the reaction to the depicted situation in which the woman figures.

But Scruton's explanation of how desires can be entertained is more elusive than revealing. For it is not clear what is withdrawn in entertaining a desire unasserted, analogous to the way the attitude of assent or belief is withdrawn in entertaining a thought unasserted. Moreover, I think that it is misleading to try to search for an unasserted analogue of a desire independently of the belief which gives rise to the desire. For there is no precise way of specifying the desire without relating it to the belief. It is in terms of the (asserted) thought underlying the belief that the desire can be identified and classified as a particular desire.[12] The total content of a desire is, roughly speaking, a thought and a feeling or reactive tendency. What the reactive tendency is directed to is determined by the attached thought—which is another way of saying that the desire is dependent on this thought. For example, if Mary desires to take Smith to task for his irresponsibility, then it follows that her desire can be identified in terms of the thought that Smith is to be reprimanded for his

[12] The thesis that desires are thought-dependent is discussed both by Wollheim and Neu. See Wollheim, 1967–8, pp. 17–24; Neu, 1977, pp. 43–5.

irresponsibility. Mary's affective mental state is dependent on this thought in so far as this thought specifies what particular desire she experiences.

The thought underlying Mary's desire is a belief. It is her belief that Smith is irresponsible that gives rise to the desire to take him to task. Thus the thought-content of the desire is the content of a belief, with which the desire is conceptually-cum-causally related. As such, if Mary's mental state is transformed from belief to 'unbelief'—that is to say, if the thought underlying the belief is as it were rendered unasserted—it would naturally be expected that the affective state or attitude that characterizes Mary's present state of mind undergoes some kind of modification. And exactly what kind of modification her mental state undergoes is the key question here. It is an answer to this very question, I think, that Scruton has been looking for.

In one sense Mary's mental state might change quite drastically. That is, if she were to realize that her belief about Smith's conduct or attitude was mistaken, then the change of her attitude from belief to unbelief would bring about the cessation of her desire to reprimand him. (Instead she might feel the desire to apologize.) But this is not what Scruton is concerned with. Rather he is claiming that even when Mary does not believe that Smith is irresponsible but merely entertains the thought that he is, she may come to feel *imaginatively* the desire to take Smith to task. And it is precisely with this point that Scruton's account leaves us perplexed. For it is not spelled out what it is to feel a desire imaginatively as opposed to feeling a desire actually—that is, as a result of having the appropriate belief.

In real life if we feel an emotion E then we also feel the desire to $\emptyset$ in response to E. This desire is, in part, produced by the belief on which E is founded. Other things being equal, we shall engage in an appropriate action A, and A will satisfy our desire. For instance, if we feel frightened by a psychopath who, we believe, is trying to strangle us, then we shall feel the desire to avoid him or take preventive measures against him. But if we merely entertain the thought of a psychopath attempting to strangle us, no desire to avoid him or prevent him from touching us will occur. The absence of the belief will render our previously felt desire inoperative. However, the question is whether rendering the desire inoperative in the aforesaid way will have the consequence of emptying our state of mind of any affective or reactive tendencies.

If rendering a desire inoperative means extinction of the desire, then the notion of 'asserted' or 'unasserted' desire is meaningless.

But if it means that, although the person does not have the desire actually to engage in some appropriate action, he is so disposed by the unasserted thought that he feels *as if* he desires to act in a certain way, then 'unasserted' desire signifies the occurrence of a reactive experience, which is explained by reference to its 'asserted counterpart'. The reactive experience is a tendency to feel inclined to act in a certain way in which he would actually act in response to a desire. But the felt inclination is essentially held back from realizing itself in the act. Perhaps Scruton wants to say that it is this affectively charged reactive tendency that makes an aesthetic experience more than the expression of a mere thought. To this claim he seems to add that the evidence for the existence of this reactive tendency is provided by certain 'passive' symptoms, which are manifested in the behaviour of the person who feels an aesthetic emotion. For example, if he feels fear towards a fictionally depicted object or scene, his fear will be expressed in the passive symptoms such as trembling, sweating, palpitating, etc. That is, if we subtract from the total state of fear those elements that are expressions of the beliefs and the desires characteristic of real life fear, the remainder will be the passive symptoms of 'imagined' fear.[13]

4.4. RAISING A RADICAL DIFFICULTY

There are two central tasks that the Radical theory is designed to perform. One is to make an original contribution to the solution of the problem of the intentionality of aesthetic emotions by reference to the theory of imagination elucidated in Section 2. The other is to develop the notion of an 'imagined' emotion in terms of the difficult concept of an 'entertained' or 'unasserted' desire—such that the existence of an imagined analogue of an actual desire makes the expression of an aesthetic response more than the expression of an unasserted thought. These two tasks are interconnected in that the imagination is held to give rise to an 'entertained emotion' or an 'entertained desire' analogous to the way beliefs give rise to emotions or desires. In this section I want to examine critically, with reference to the earlier explained theory of imagination, whether Scruton's project faces any serious difficulty. I shall argue that the Radical theory contains a radical difficulty and that this difficulty stems from the theory of imagination expounded in it.

It is not my purpose to examine the tenability or otherwise of

[13] See Scruton, pp. 131–2.

Scruton's theory of imagination. But given the way it is defined and developed, my concern is whether the imagination can succeed in accomplishing its goal, namely the evocation of emotions that are merely entertained rather than acted upon. This question arises, not from the thesis that imagining and believing are essentially contrasted attitudes of mind, but from the claim that imagination can be an effective substitute for belief in the arousal of emotions. For the remark that imagination can give rise to emotion somewhat in the way belief does in real life seems to be at variance with the thesis that imagination is *essentially contrasted* with belief. It is puzzling why a thought-process governed by the imagination would not be rendered causally inefficacious in generating a genuine emotional experience, in view of the fact that the occurrence of such a thought lacks an essential property by virtue of which a thought-process governed by a belief exerts causal power needed to elicit an emotion. In other words, to draw an essential contrast between imagination and belief is also to imply that imagination is devoid of the causal dynamism which characterizes the role of a belief in the occurrence of an emotion.[14]

It may, however, be argued that aesthetic emotions are emotions only in an attenuated sense because experiencing such an emotion does not lead to any appropriate action in the way experiencing a real-life emotion does. And this difference—let us describe it as the feature of 'passivity'—may be alluded to in accounting for the essential difference drawn between imagination and belief. In other words, the point may be made that imagination is causally ineffi-cacious only in evoking full-fledged emotions that naturally result in some appropriate actions, but not inefficacious in giving rise to any emotional experience whatsoever. Thus it is not that imagination is causally impotent; rather its causal power is weaker than that of belief and, hence, can only give rise to 'passive' emotional responses to fictions.

But this argument does not make the puzzle disappear; on the contrary it makes the puzzle reappear in another form. For to

---

[14] It seems to me that Aristotle holds the same view regarding the inefficacy of mere imagination in producing emotions. Thus in *De Anima* he remarks that 'when we think something to be fearful or threatening, emotion is immediately produced, and so too with what is encouraging. But when we merely imagine we remain as unaffected as persons who are looking at a painting of some dreadful or encouraging scene'. (Book III, Chapter 3, 427b) Of course Aristotle is plainly wrong if he implies, by the last sentence, that people *never* feel any fear or encouragement as a result of watching a painting that depicts a dreadful or encouraging scene.

accept the above interpretation would imply that imagination and belief are not *essentially* contrasted states or attitudes of mind: that is, the difference between the two is not one of kind but one of degree. Evidently such an implication cannot be allowed to follow in Scruton's theory. Hence we are again required to invoke the cognitive state or attitude of belief by reference to which a causal explanation of even attenuated emotional experience is to be provided.

Perhaps Scruton would reply that the above is a *non sequitur*. He may argue that fictional emotions differ from real-life emotions in *kind*, not just in degree. Whereas real-life emotions normally are motivations for appropriate action, fictional emotions are essentially passive. And this constitutes a difference in kind, in which case their intentional causes can also differ in kind. Thus, Scruton may say that imagination can differ from belief in kind and still carry the causal load in the case of fictional emotions.

It seems to me, however, that the above remarks are rather deceptive. For granted that fictional emotions can be shown to be different in kind from their real-life counterparts by reference to action or motivation, this difference must not make us overlook the fact that there is also a significant phenomenological similarity between the two cases of emotion. For example, one can feel a deep sadness in response to a scene in a theatre or a film or to a passage in a literary work and this experience can in some respects be felt to be very similar to the experience of an analogous real life sadness. Now, the similarity of the affective quality of the two emotions calls for a corresponding similarity in their intentional causes. There must at least be some common factor between the two causes and it is such a common factor which will explain the similarity of the responses.

Even when a fictional emotion does not force itself upon us with great intensity, it is still a genuine emotional response and not just a fake simulacrum of a real-life emotion. Indeed, Scruton himself emphasizes the 'necessary continuity' between fictional emotions and real-life emotions and argues, by citing the case of fictional sadness, that 'to find a work of art sad is to respond to it in the way I respond to a man when I am 'touched' by his sadness'. (Scruton, 1974, p. 72) It is this similarity in the 'intentional stance' towards a work of fiction that accounts for the genuineness of an emotional response to a fictional object. This in turn indicates that the intentional cause of an emotional response to fiction must be sufficiently similar to the intentional cause of an emotional response to some analogous real-life situation.

But what common generative condition can be shared by belief and imagination if they are held to represent essentially contrasted attitudes of mind? Although belief and imagination can represent the same thought-content about something, it would be wrong to conclude from this intentional isomorphism that they are also causally similar. For it is the assertedness of a thought that endows the relevant mental state with its causal dynamism. It is a distinct psychological attitude that the thought involves with regard to the object referred to by the thought, thereby 'activating' the mental state with a certain affective disposition towards the object. But to say that even a thought, which is intentionally isomorphic with an asserted thought but which is itself not asserted, can likewise be effective in evoking a similar affective disposition towards a fictional situation is, I think, to undermine the very thesis that the corresponding mental states or attitudes, namely imagination and belief, are necessarily contrasted.

Hence we are again required to invoke the cognitive state or attitude of belief by reference to which a causal explanation of even attenuated emotional experiences is to be provided. But such an experience consists of the reactive tendency that remains when the characteristic belief and desire are subtracted from a full-fledged emotion. Therefore it seems impossible to refer to any full-blooded belief in order to account for the affective experience. And we have found that having recourse to anything like a quasi-belief is nothing but an abortive attempt to solve the puzzle.

Since imagination is indifferent to truth or the referential considerations of the underlying thought, the mental state of imagination can be characterized as a state or attitude of 'unbelief'. To be in a state of 'unbelief', or to entertain the attitude of 'unbelief', is not to be concerned with whether the thought represented by that state of mind refers to anything actual. Thus our thinking carried out in imagination is essentially existentially uncommitted. Furthermore, and more importantly, from the standpoint of the imaginer the thought in which his imagination consists is apprehended in an uncommitted or hypothetical frame of mind. That is to say, to maintain an attitude of 'unbelief' towards what one imagines is to dwell on the thought *for its own sake*; for there is nothing in reality that the thought is about.

Contrasted with the above case, a person who thinks about something by believing in it dwells upon the thought not for its own sake but for the sake of what it refers to. The thought is as it were harboured in a committed or categorical frame of mind. As such, the thought naturally exerts an influence on the person, whereby he is disposed to adjust himself in a certain way with regard to what the thought is about. Nowhere else is this influence of thought more conspicuous than in the case of an emotion, where the thought is foundational to the existence of the emotion. In other words, evaluative beliefs that are involved in emotions are essentially constituted of committed apprehensions of some aspects of reality. If the person apprehends that something has such and such a property, or set of properties, this apprehension immediately commits him to adjust himself in some appropriate ways with respect to whatever object or situation is in question. And this adjustment consists of two layers. On the one hand, he is so to speak thrown into an affective state; on the other hand, this affective state creates the inclination for a certain type of action or behaviour. Thus the belief from which this complex form of adjustment issues can be said to be charged with a causal dynamism—a property that may be described as intrinsic to the nature of such beliefs.

For example, the person's committed apprehension that an enraged lion standing in front of him is threateningly dangerous puts him in a certain affective mode called 'fear'. He is then inclined to do somethings to avoid the lion, or protect himself against its attack. Other things being equal, he engages in some appropriate action towards which his inclination points. Given ordinary characteristics of human nature, he is apt to feel committed to adjust himself in this way. And his whole existential condition, including the strategy that he adopts, can be said to be triggered off by this belief. It is an essential property of the belief that it brings about a specific type of modification of the person's mental state and his adaptation to a new situation. Hence the belief is a causal condition of the emotion and the appropriate action or behaviour that follows from the emotion.

It follows from the above that to subtract the belief on which a particular emotion is founded is to eliminate the causal condition of the emotion. As we have already seen in Chapter One, the abandonment of the belief normally results in the extinction or the gradual cessation of the emotion that includes the belief. Now, if someone were merely to entertain the thought of something fictitious—such as the thought of an enraged lion that might occur when seeing a statue or plastic fabrication—the mental process that carries his thought would not include the causal condition needed to arouse

the emotion, namely fear. This means that the thought entertained
by him would lack causal dynamism and he would not be disposed to
feel the emotion or act in a certain way towards the object as dictated
by the emotion. And this is roughly what it means to be in a state of
'unbelief'. Thus, merely imagining the object, or entertaining the
thought of it in an attitude of unbelief, cannot lead the imaginer to
have an emotional experience that is analogous to the emotion
which he would feel towards the object were he to believe in its
existence.

In response to my above argument, Scruton might say that there
is no a priori reason why imagination cannot be construed as a causally
efficacious state of mind. He might argue that imagination is possessed
of a different kind of causal dynamism and, hence, is able to give
rise to a somewhat different kind of emotional experience. That is
to say, imagination has causal power of its own kind and this power
is exerted in the evocation of 'passive' emotional responses to works
of art.

But the above response endows the imagination with the property
of emotion-evoking causal efficacy in a rather mysterious way. For
it is quite unclear how an attitude that uses the imagination can
embody the capacity to generate an affective disposition towards
the object *if* the thought is characterized by a total indifference to
what it refers to, or to what it might be about. The attitude of total
indifference to the truth (or falsity) of the thought renders imagination deficient as a causal factor in the production of emotions.

Someone might then object that the imagination embodies a
causal capacity by virtue of making the imaginer think of the real
counterpart of the imagined scene and thereby making him feel the
relevant emotion. But this would imply that what he feels towards
the object is not due to mere imagination but to the association of
ideas that imagination brings in its train. And this would not be
consistent with Scruton's theory. Indeed, since the associated ideas
would be related to real-life contexts, their entry into the 'imaginative'
thought-process would be tantamount to the infiltration of full-
blooded beliefs.

Thus the above considerations reinforce the impression that the
occurrence of emotions even in 'passive' form needs to be accounted
for by reference to appropriate beliefs or some sort of mental states
tinged with belief. Imagination, as expounded in the Radical
theory, cannot incorporate belief or be tinged with belief. Hence
the theory of aesthetic emotions put forward as a radical proposal

turns out to be untenable. It is necessary that our attitude to works of art or fiction be partly an attitude of unasserted thought or unbelief, since what is represented in such works is known to be fictional. Therefore the role of imagination is partially constitutive of the aesthetic attitude. But it is only *partially* constitutive, and the task now is to identify the remaining part or parts.

The discussion of this chapter confirms the view that the exact role of belief in fictional emotions is difficult to establish. While no theory attempting to delineate the concept of a second-order belief or quasi-belief is able to incorporate the causal condition necessary to explain the occurrence of fictional emotions, recourse to a theory of imagination that dispenses with belief altogether is also found to be subject to the same failure. Thus our investigation seems to have completed a full circle. It started off with the need for belief to secure the intentionality and causation of fictional emotions. It then ran through theories of belief of a different order based on first-order belief. Next, it examined a project which tries to eliminate belief altogether so as to establish the thesis of a new order of inten-tionality and causation, by which the genesis of a 'passive' emotional response to fiction is to be explained. It has now left us again with the feeling that somehow a role for belief proper must be acknow-ledged in the constitution of fictional emotions.

CHAPTER FIVE

THE CONSERVATIVE THEORY:
A NEW PROPOSAL

Having recognized that neither the reformist nor the radical campaign is able to provide the causal conditions needed to explain the occurrence of fictional emotions, we might feel inclined to have recourse to a conservative policy. This policy advocates a re-evaluation of the issue with the explicit purpose of accounting for fictional emotions within the framework of the standard form of intentionality, that is in terms of belief proper. In this chapter I shall follow up this intuition and try to set forth a new theory which makes provision for an explanation of the causation of fictional emotions by reference to belief. Since my aim here is to 'conserve' the old form of intentionality, with some qualifications added to it, I shall entitle my proposal 'the Conservative theory'.

However, it would be wrong to conclude that nothing substantial will be incorporated in this theory from the Reformist and the Radical theories. For what I intend to do in developing the Conservative theory is twofold. On the one hand I want to retain the *spirit* of the Reformist theory by aiming to give a causal explanation of fictional emotions by reference to belief, but without postulating any notion of an 'extended' belief, or belief of a different order. On the other hand I want to follow the *direction* of the Radical theory by preserving the theory that imagination is a species of unasserted thought, without thereby preventing the infiltration of belief or asserted thought into aesthetic responses or emotional responses to fiction. It is hoped that when the 'reformist spirit' and the 'radical direction' are rightly synthesized, the result will be a more satisfactory analysis of the structure of aesthetic or fictional emotions. Furthermore, by according belief its legitimate place, along with the imagination, within that structure, it will also establish the rationality of emotional responses to fiction, thereby providing an answer to Radford's objection.

5.1. EMOTION, PARADIGMATIC EVALUATION AND CAUSATION

To unfold the structure of emotional responses to fiction is primarily to describe the conditions that are necessarily involved in experiencing such an emotion. The task is, to use Kantian terminology, to bring to light the conditions of the possibility of such an emotional experience. And to do this we need to inquire into the logical structure of the thought-process that the subject of these emotions undergoes. We have to determine the way he must think about the fictional object which is represented in a work of fiction, so that he can come to experience some particular emotion through this mode of thought.

The project undertaken in Chapter One was principally to examine the conceptual structure of the thought-process that underlies real-life emotions. Thus it is against the background of the conclusions of that chapter that our present inquiry into the logical structure of the thought-process underlying fictional emotions has to be carried on. It is the 'fictionality' (or 'aestheticity' in Scruton's sense) of these emotions that raises the need for an alternative account of their structure. But the alternative account must not depart too far from the paradigmatic account if the former is to count as a structural description of *emotion*. That is to say, there must be some common condition for the possibility both of fictional and of real-life emotions. And it is by virtue of the satisfaction of this common condition that the essential continuity between the two is preserved.

Here is a recapitulation of the structural description of a real-life emotion. In feeling an emotion directed towards an existing object, one has a specific thought of the object and is in an affective state based on this thought. This thought essentially amounts to an evaluative belief, and this belief is both rationally and causally related to the affective state. In other words, the evaluative belief, along with the existential belief about the object, is the rational and causal foundation of the emotion. Thus the analysis of an emotion requires identifying the thought or belief necessarily included in it. Emotions can thus be partially characterized as modes of believing certain propositions about their objects.

To the extent that an emotion is a way of believing a proposition about its object, it can also be said that the thought-process underlying the experience occurs under a description. And the description under which the thought occurs specifies the appropriate belief that is necessary for the emotion to be possible. For example, if I am angry with you because I believe that you have put me in trouble by playing a malignantly deceptive game, the thought-process undergone by me in experiencing this anger occurs under the description 'You have done an injustice to me'. This description captures the belief which partially constitutes my mental state of anger. I believe that what you have done to me is unfair. My anger grows out of this belief. Such a description characterizes what might be called an *evaluative paradigm*, in terms of which your action or attitude is judged. Hence the belief captured by the description is an evaluative belief, which governs my thought and gives rise to an affective state.

Not only do I have the evaluative belief that you have done me an injustice, but I also have the existential belief that there is someone who has actually harmed me in the afore-described way and that you are that person. Thus my anger is constituted by two layers of belief—the existential and the evaluative—as we already discussed in Chapter One. In judging your action or attitude in the light of an evaluative paradigm I also perceive, and thus believe, that you exist as the object of my anger.

It might be said that the involvement of the existential belief is too obvious and insignificant to be worth mentioning. Doubt might be cast on whether the idea of an existential belief plays any conceptually essential role in the analysis of the structure of emotions. But, as will become apparent, it is precisely due to overlooking the importance of what is so obvious that various attempts to account for fictional emotions have resulted in untenable theories. I want to argue that it is only by taking the distinction between evaluative and existential beliefs seriously that we can resolve the puzzles and paradoxes encountered by many philosophers.

When we come to consider fictional emotions in the light of the belief structure of real-life emotions, it becomes immediately evident that the former occur in the absence of existential beliefs. It is precisely because they occur in the absence of existential beliefs that it is appropriate to describe them as *fictional* emotions. A fictional emotion is directed towards some object or event that is merely depicted as existing. To appreciate the intentionality of the depiction is somehow to construct the object or event in the imagination. And it is because the emotion occurs in an existential vacuum, as it were, that we are required to describe it as founded on imagination. The subject fills in the void, created by the absence of the existential belief, by means of the imagination. The imagination is made to play an alternative conceptual role in place of the existential belief. The fictional object or event is 'created' by an attitude of mind that is essentially contrasted with the attitude of existential belief.

At this point it would be appropriate to revert to the theory of imagination expounded by Scruton and connect it with the remarks made in the above passage. Scruton's claim that the imagination is essentially contrasted with belief can now be better understood in terms of the distinction that has been made between existential and evaluative beliefs. What the claim actually means, I want to argue, is that only existential beliefs are essentially contrasted with the imagination. For what makes the contrast possible is the difference of attitude in which the two thought-processes are related to their respective objects. And this difference is explicable by reference to the concept of existential commitment. It is an analytic consequence of believing in the existence of some particular thing or state of affairs that the believer is existentially committed to the thing or state of affairs. Thus the thought-process involved in an existential belief carries with it the attitude of assent to the actuality of the object or situation. But when someone imagines something or some event, it in no way follows that the thought-process of the imaginer must include the attitude of assent to the actuality of the object or event imagined. Indeed it is part of the concept of imagination that one be able to imagine something independently of whether it is believed to exist or not. There is no existential tie binding imagination to reality.

What I want to underline here is that the relation between imagination and evaluative beliefs has to be construed in a quite different way. For the nature and content of evaluative beliefs are such that to have such a belief does not amount to adopting an attitude not consonant with the attitude of imagination. On the contrary, the two attitudes are perfectly compatible. Basically, evaluative beliefs consist of certain appraisive frameworks in terms of which the subject interprets the world in relation to himself. And it is objects and events of his existential beliefs that are so interpreted. These objects, events or states of affairs are apprehended *as* replete with certain aspects or properties. From the standpoint of the human agent, such an estimative conceptualization of situations evaluatively changes the world from what it would otherwise have been: that is a world of mere existential beliefs.

Now I want to put forward two contentions which are of central importance to the proposed Conservative theory. The first is that fictional emotions occur through the combined operation of imagination, and evaluative beliefs. Whereas in the absence of an existential belief the imagination fills its role in the constitution of a fictional emotion, there is no corresponding absence of an evaluative belief in this constitution. On the contrary, the thought-process involved in experiencing a particular fictional emotion is guided by the same evaluative belief that regulates the occurrence of the corresponding real-life emotion. That is to say, while the role of the existential belief in a particular real-life emotion is replaced by the role of the imagination, in the case of the fictional counterpart of that emotion, the regulative, paradigmatic function of the evaluative belief is not superseded by any other attitude of mind in the fictional case . Thus, in so far as their belief structure is concerned, real-life and fictional emotions differ only in the existential dimension of this structure; in the evaluative dimension the two are characteristically the same.

A concrete example will help explain the above argument in detail. For the sake of simplicity let us take the case of a fear produced by the sight of an enraged lion depicted in a painting or a film, and let us name it'fictional fear'. If someone feels this fear, then evidently his mental state at that time is not founded on the existential belief that there is an enraged lion, since there is only a painted canvas, or a film screen, on which the image of an enraged lion is depicted or reflected. Therefore he imagines, or entertains in thought, the existence of an enraged lion standing before him. To this extent his mental state has its basis in imagination. But in 'creating' the fictional existence of the enraged lion the imagination also acts in conformity with an evaluative paradigm that is conceptually tied to his understanding of some salient aspect of an enraged lion. In other words, it is on the basis of his knowledge about the strength of such an animal and its likely behaviour towards human beings in certain circumstances that he perceives the lion as a 'dangerous object'. He does believe it to be a threat to his life. And imagining the existence of it in front of him, he is also thinking of what he imagines in terms of the property of dangerousness, though he is not threatened by what he watches to the extent of taking precautionary measures against it.

The evaluative belief about the dangerousness of enraged lions is integral to the constitution of the total mental state of fictionally fearing the depicted enraged lion. For the thought-process involved in having this fear is as much governed by the appropriate evaluative belief as is the thought-process underlying a real-life fear of an enraged lion. Thus there is the same regulative conception, encapsulated in the description 'enraged lions are dangerous', under which the mental processes both of fictional fear and of real-life fear occur. Indeed, that his imaginative thought-process occurs under this description is a necessary condition of the possibility of his feeling fictional fear.

My second contention is that it is by reference to the evaluative belief, and not by reference to the existential belief, that the formal object of an emotion is specified. If the formal object of fear is 'something dangerous' then it is the evaluative belief which appraises the object in question and recognizes it as a kind of object that has the property of being dangerous. That is to say, the formal object of fear results, not so much from the belief that, say, an enraged lion is standing in front of someone, as from the belief that this lion is very likely to cause irreparable harm to him. The object of the existential belief, as it were, awaits an evaluative assessment before it can be recognized or appreciated as the sort of entity or event which can be, e.g. feared, envied, regretted, admired, pitied, or treated with anger, contempt, or indignation. The object is then classified under some emotion-relevant property.

In developing the Radical theory of fictional emotions, Scruton maintains the mistaken view that emotional responses to works of art do not have formal objects in the way emotions, and responses in general, have. His argument is that if emotions acquire formal objects in virtue of their being founded on appropriate beliefs, emotional responses to works of art, which are not founded on beliefs, cannot acquire formal objects. (Scruton, pp. 71–7) For example, if one is saddened by a poor waif depicted in a painting as a result of imagining the actuality of the depicted scene, one does not believe that there really is a poor-looking waif in a situation which is both unfortunate and regrettable. Thus, assuming that the formal object of sadness is 'a situation which is viewed as both unfortunate and regrettable', one's response of sadness to the waif cannot be said to acquire the formal object of sadness in that one does not believe that the situation depicted in the painting actually exists.

The mistake in the above view is apparent: it stems from the failure to distinguish between existential beliefs and evaluative beliefs. Although it is true that there is no situation which one believes to be unfortunate and regrettable when one responds to the waif in the above example, it does not follow that any description of his experience has to be given without mentioning the formal object of sadness. After all, the situation which is imagined and towards which one feels sadness is appreciated in terms of the features specified by the formal object of sadness. In other words, the depicted situation is viewed (imaginatively) as unfortunate and regrettable; and it is because the situation is viewed in this way that one responds to it with sadness. Hence aesthetic emotions, or emotional responses to fiction, cannot be described without mentioning their formal objects.

What is surely lacking, in the above example, is the existential belief that there is a waif in the afore-described condition; and to this extent one's sadness towards the waif is not based on belief. But it is not from this belief that the formal object of sadness, in this case, results. Rather, it is the belief about what makes a situation saddening that allows one to view the depicted situation of the poor-looking waif as unfortunate and regrettable. And the evaluative belief provides the criteria of this appraisal of the waif's condition.

Having made both these contentions, I now have to show how fictional emotions actually occur as a result of the combination of imagination and evaluative beliefs. More precisely, what I have to consider is the causation of fictional emotions. I pointed out in Chapter One that beliefs play a causal role in eliciting emotions. Normally, it is the combination of an existential belief and an appropriate evaluative belief that suffices to exert the causal force needed to produce a particular real-life emotion. The question now is: How does the replacement of the existential belief by the imagination affect the original causal dynamism?

One view might be that the abandonment of the existential belief would lead to a breakdown of the original causal transmission, implying thereby that this belief is crucial to the actual operation of the causal dynamo. Why should someone feel an emotion E towards an object or event O if he does not believe O to be actual, even though he possesses the appropriate evaluative belief about the E-relevant properties of the actual counterpart of O? That is to say, why isn't the evaluative belief causally otiose when it is dissociated from the existential belief?

This negative response overlooks the fact that in the fictional case the evaluative belief does not have to exert a causal influence *by itself* in order to give rise to an emotion. The evaluative belief is supplemented by the imagination and the combination of the two is sufficient. The evaluative belief does not, so to speak, idle, but gets applied to a 'content' provided by the imagination. And this content is the same as that provided by the existential belief in the corresponding real-life emotion. For what is imagined to exist in this case is precisely that which is normally believed to exist.

However, the objection might still be continued. For it could be argued that the subject's state of mind is now described as containing a conflicting pair of attitudes, namely an asserted thought—i.e. the thought underlying the evaluative belief, and an unasserted thought—i.e. the thought of the fictional object. The existence of mutually conflicting attitudes in the same mental state probably would make the operation of the required causation impossible. Hence, if the objection were correct , the combination of an evaluative belief and an unasserted thought could not constitute a causally efficacious state of mind that gives rise to an emotion.

The importance of this objection is undeniable in that it forces us to scrutinize the complexity of the combination in question. Nevertheless, the objection is not fatal because the alleged conflict is not actually there. The conflict appears only if the elements of the combination are considered severally. But the fact of the matter is that the two elements are not merely juxtaposed. Rather, they are united in a unique frame of mind in such a way that the unasserted thought is, as it were, 'saturated' by the evaluative belief. Being so saturated, this thought or thought-process is no longer constitutive of a mental state that carries a purely fictitious content, as it would be if the total thought-complex were divested of the evaluative belief. For there is nothing fictional about the content of the evaluative belief. On the contrary this belief is true in a paradigmatic sense in so far as it is by reference to suitable evaluative beliefs that actual events or states of affairs are perceived or appraised.

The above argument is that when the unasserted thought about a fictional object is entertained in a frame of mind which primarily embraces the appropriate evaluative belief, what is otherwise counted as merely fictional is then deemed to be a possibility, or, in Aristotle's words, 'what is capable of happening according to the rule of probability or necessity'. (Aristotle, 1967, Ch. 9, 1451, p. 32) Once the evaluative belief so permeates the unasserted thought, the fictional content of the imaginative thought-process is provided with a real-life context—a context from which the fictional description derives its connotation. And as a consequence of this peculiar interaction, the fictionality of what is imagined is set aside, thereby letting the subject concentrate his attention on the sense or significance of the unasserted thought. When the fictionality of the fictional thought is so 'bracketed out', its content is appreciated as having the sense or significance that makes the thought akin to a thought about an analogous real-life situation. And it is this recognition of kinship with, or relevance to, real life that triggers off the disposition to respond emotionally to the fictional situation in the way, to some extent, one is disposed towards its actual counterpart.

An objection may be raised that my account of the combination of the unasserted thought and the evaluative belief is couched too densely in the metaphors of 'saturation' and 'permeation' and that these metaphors need to be spelt out. But it seems to me that recourse to metaphor is extremely difficult to avoid in giving an explanation of this complex phenomenon. And it is not just that the fictional context has this complexity; the character of the combination of an existential belief and a relevant evaluative belief in a real-life context is no less complex. For even in this context we seem to be constrained to say that the existential belief is 'saturated' with, or 'permeated' by, the relevant evaluative belief. For example, if I am afraid of swimming in a particular lake because I believe that there is a poisonous snake in it, then I believe there to be something dangerous, which I desire to avoid at all cost. Now it seems no distortion of fact to say that my belief that there is a poisonous snake here is saturated by the evaluative belief that poisonous snakes are dangerous to us. The use of the metaphor is intended to highlight the point about how our evaluative beliefs determine our perception of the world and our consequent response to the world. The aforesaid combination is not merely a matter of contingent conjunction, but more intimate, so as to be faithfully described by the metaphor of saturation.

5.2. EMOTION WITHOUT ACTION

The causal explanation provided thus far does not, however, say anything about the distinguishing features in terms of which fictional emotions are significantly differentiated from analogous real-life emotions. Certainly the combined force of an evaluative belief and an existential belief is normally going to be much stronger in the elicitation of an emotion than the causal force generated by the union of an evaluative belief and an unasserted thought. It is generally true, for instance, that our fear of an enraged lion encountered in a forest is of much greater intensity than our fear evoked by the sight of an enraged lion depicted in a work of fiction. What is of importance in this connection is how we respond to our emotion in both cases, and how the philosophical explanation given in Section 5.1. can account for the difference in these responses.

Real-life emotions, in general, are also motives to action. We classify emotions not arbitrarily but according to their role in the explanation of behaviour. As motives they are intermediary between belief (or better the combination of evaluative and existential beliefs) and action. Thus they give rise to specific desires, and the desires occasion appropriate actions. In Chapter Four we discussed how an emotion is normally explicable in terms of a belief and a desire united in a causal-cum-conceptual relation. Jealousy seeks not just to interpret the world but also elicits the desire to change it, which in turn might actually engage the jealous person in some appropriate act that brings about the desired end. Anger is not just the belief that someone has done an injustice, but also embodies the desire to punish the unjust person. Similarly, my fear of the enraged lion is not merely founded on the belief that it is dangerous, but also generative of the desire to avoid it.[1]

Thus it is possible to give an extended analysis of real-life emotions in terms of a tripartite relation of belief, desire and action. The belief that the ferocious lion in front of me is dangerous causes fear in me. I am affected in certain ways: I turn pale, tremble, my heartbeat increases and I feel a sensation of tightness in my stomach. The desire to run away from the lion, or to prevent it from coming towards me, grows strongly. If there is no particular impediment to my being able to run away, or protect myself from the lion, then the next thing I do is act in accordance with my desire. Either I run away or try to defend myself against an impending attack. Stemming from the belief and enduring with the belief, my fear comes to a completion in an appropriate action.

Now, if we are to apply the tripartite framework in a similar analysis of fictional emotions, we must provide analogues of these three elements. Earlier I mentioned that the analogue of belief in the fictional case is an unasserted thought. And it is to be remembered that the unasserted thought is an analogue of the existential belief, not of the evaluative belief. The analogue of desire, to repeat, is an 'unasserted' tendency or disposition to act or behave in a certain way. It was also stated that there cannot be an imagined analogue of action, since a fictional emotion does not commit the subject to adopt an appropriate action-strategy in the way a real-life emotion does. Of course the subject might be motivated to adopt such a strategy in the imagination; but the object of his emotion being

---

[1] As Robert Solomon writes: 'Emotions are laden with *intentions to act*. Emotions are concerned not only with 'the way the world is' but with the way the world *ought* to be. Every emotion, in other words, is also a personal ideology, a projection into the future, and a system of hopes and desires, expectations and commitments, intentions and strategies for changing our world'. (Solomon, 1977, p. 212, italics in the original)

fictional, the strategy would not materialize in an action which can be said non-metaphorically to concern *that* object. For instance, a fictional anger is an emotion directed towards a fictional person. One can envisage punishing the person; but no actual act of punishment can thereby occur which can be identified as punishing *that* person. As such, fictional emotions are aptly characterizable as emotions *without* action.[2]

It is this idea of an emotion without action that needs to be explained by reference to the complex notion of an 'unasserted' desire or disposition to act in a specific way. In Chapter Four I tried to analyse the complexity of what it is to 'entertain' a desire. But the analysis was scant in view of the magnitude of the issue. Hence I shall attempt an elaboration of what was adumbrated in that analysis. In essence, there is a twofold question to which I need to address myself: How does such an 'unasserted' desire occur, and what accounts for its essential untranslatability into action? For the sake of explanatory simplicity, I shall revert once again to the example of feeling fear towards an enraged lion depicted in a work of art, and provide answers to the above question.

Though our fear of the depicted enraged lion is not accompanied by the actual desire to avoid it, we still experience the inclination to act in a certain way—in the way we normally act in response to an actual desire arising from a real-life fear for an enraged lion. Some such reactive experience does occur in us, and it is the presence of this experience which makes our mental state affectively charged. And what disposes us to feel inclined in this way is the unique coalescence of the evaluative belief that enraged lions are dangerous and the entertainment of a thought about such a lion existing in front of us. When the unasserted thought about such a lion occurs under the regulative conception that lions of this character are in general dangerous or a threat to one's life, a reactive attitude is spontaneously generated in our mind even towards the imagined lion. The pattern of this reactive feeling is analogous to the actual desire that we would feel were we to encounter the imagined situation.

However, since we are also aware of the fact that this is an imagined predicament, and not an existential predicament, the felt inclination is essentially held back from realizing itself in some appropriate act

---

[2] Of course any kind of action might occur in response to the fictional situation. For example, an audience watching a fictional performance of a horror story might be so affected as to leave the theatre, or throw something on to the stage or screen. But such actions are not *appropriate* actions with respect to the situation depicted.

that typically results from the desire to avoid an enraged lion. More precisely, it is the absence of the existential belief that accounts for the suspended nature of our reactive tendency. The peculiarity of fictional fears is such that while we feel somewhat activated to engage in some appropriate action, at the same time our urge to do so is immediately impeded due to our implicit recognition that the relevant existential belief is missing.[3] Indeed, it would not be wrong to say that the nature of our fear of the depicted enraged lion is aptly describable in terms that attribute some sort of indeterminacy to the state of mind: that is, we are left in a state of *stirred inactivity*. It is in this sense that a kind of 'passivity' or 'inactivity' can be ascribed to fictional emotions as one of the essential marks.

5.3. MERE THINKING, ENVISAGEMENT AND EMOTION

I have not yet questioned whether the theory elucidated thus far provides both necessary and sufficient conditions for the possibility of fictional emotions. It might be wondered, in particular, whether the combination of the evaluative belief and the unasserted thought is sufficient to elicit an emotional response towards something

[3] But recognizing that the existential belief is absent does not mean that the unasserted thought has been 'unsaturated' and the imagination has resumed its place. For the imagination is part of the structure of the entire process and, therefore, the unassertedness of the thought is integral to this process. And to say that the imaginative thought is 'saturated' and the fictionality in question is 'bracketed out' is not to imply that the fact about the absence of the existential belief is temporarily forgotten. The point is that the imagination does not replace the existential belief in the structure of a fictional emotion; it merely plays an alternative role so as to 'construct' the existence of the object in thought.

The remarks made above, and the argument presented in the text, can be compared with the views of an eighteenth century literary critic and playwright, William Kenrick. In his criticism of Dr Samuel Johnson's *Preface to The Plays of William Shakespeare*, Kenrick writes:

The spectator is unquestionably deceived, but the deception goes no further than the passions, it affects our sensibility but not our understanding; and is by no means so powerful a delusion as to affect our *belief*. There is a species of probability which is necessary to be adhered to, even to engage the attention of the senses and affect our passions; but this regards the *representation* and not the *materiality* of the fable. (Kenrick, 1765 in Vickers (ed.), 1979, p. 191)

Talk about 'deception' in the above-quote passage must not be mistaken to refer to some sort of half-believed or semi-deluded state of mind, but only to the work of the imagination 'to engage the attention of the senses' to the depicted scenario. This imaginative activity, howsoever effective it might be to our sensibility, does not blind the understanding to the absence of the existential belief.

fictional. For example, suppose that an art critic watches a performance of *Othello* along with another person. It seems possible for them to hold the same evaluative belief about Desdemona's plight and entertain the same unasserted thought—namely that Desdemona has been suffocated to death by her inordinately jealous husband, and yet differ in the way they respond to what they watch. While the ordinary member—let us call him Robinson—responds to Desdemona with deep sadness and finds himself with tearful eyes, the critic—let us call him Johnson—expresses no emotion at all. Is there then a third element which accounts for Robinson's emotional response to the fictional woman and Johnson's unemotional appreciation of the plight of the woman?

The usual answer to the above question, I think, would be that Johnson is watching the fictional performance with a kind of aesthetic detachment, which prevents him from *empathizing* with the fictional character. Unlike Robinson, he has not 'entered into' the fictional world in which Desdemona suffers a tragic end of her life. On the other hand, Robinson is said to have empathized with her by somehow descending to the world of the *dramatis persona*. His unasserted thought about Desdemona includes an empathetic attitude towards her, whereas Johnson's unasserted thought excludes such an attitude by the resolute adoption of a sense of neutrality. Thus, it may be said, this lack of empathy impedes the evaluative belief from causally charging the unasserted thought in order to evoke sadness or some such feeling. Empathy, then, is what must be added to the other two elements so as to provide the sufficient condition.

The inclusion of an unqualified notion of empathy in the explanation of fictional emotions is undesirable, however, because it begs the question. The statement that someone empathizes with Desdemona entails an emotion-sentence, namely that he feels a certain emotion towards her. Hence the addition of empathy to the combination of the other two factors does not yield a non-circular explanation of fictional emotions. We must therefore attempt to provide an explanation that is independent of any reference to emotion or emotion-laden mental attitudes.

In order to find an independent explanation, we should ask whether Robinson and Johnson really do hold the same evaluative belief(s) and the same unasserted thoughts with respect to both *form* and *content*. A closer scrutiny is called for to find out if the apparent identity of the propositional structure of what they hold masks a significant discrepancy in the representational contents of their thoughts. Both viewers may be said to have one and the same evaluative belief in that it is the same proposition, or the same set of propositions, which each holds. Similarly, both may be taken to be entertaining the same unasserted thought in that it is the same proposition that underlies their respective thought-processes. And yet on either score each may still be importantly different. The same evaluative belief may figure in Robinson's mind as possessed of relatively greater strength or seriousness, whereas it may figure in Johnson's mind as possessed of lesser strength or seriousness.[4] Likewise, the same unasserted thought, which is entertained by both, may in fact amount to substantially different intentional acts or states in the two minds. The intentional or representational content of the thought, as it emerges in Robinson's mental process, may include certain phenomenological features that are absent in the intentional content of the thought as it arises in Johnson's mental process.

However, the alleged scepticism with respect to the similarity of the evaluative beliefs, held by these two people, can be allayed. For it is conceivable that two people hold the same evaluative belief—in the sense of assenting to the same proposition, or the same set of propositions—and also that each attaches more or less the same importance to what he believes, feeling roughly the same impact of the belief. This similarity could be interpreted in terms of some paradigm that sets the criteria for the evaluation of the situation in question. And it is the same paradigm that is the common basis of the two people's evaluative beliefs. Let us assume that Robinson and Johnson are in this equilibrium position. Granted this, our attention should then be directed to the alleged scepticism about the identity or non-identity between the relevant unasserted thoughts. Is the unasserted thought that Johnson entertains about Desdemona's fate really the same as the one that Robinson entertains about the same object? Apparently it is one and the same, in that it is *the thought of Desdemona's fate*. There are certain descriptions, specified in the play, which depict the fate of Desdemona, and it is this set of descriptions that is commonly true of their thoughts. Thus, there are constraints, imposed by the text of the play, on what sort of thought they both can entertain.

Nevertheless, the identity of the descriptions of *what* thought they entertain must not be confused with the identity of the descriptions of *how* each of them actually entertains the thought. That

---

[4] The strength of a belief is determined by the extent to which the belief motivates the believer to act or feel in certain ways.

is to say, the way each of them entertains the same unasserted thought can vary phenomenologically. Here I want to claim that it is due to this variation that Robinson and Johnson are subjects of significantly different intentional states. Although it is Desdemona's fate about which Johnson entertains an unasserted thought, the way he lets this thought figure in his mind is characteristically unlike the way Robinson's disposition leads the thought to figure in his mind.

Johnson holds before his mind the unasserted thought of Desdemona's fate somewhat in the way one holds an unasserted thought of something that figures in the if-clause of an 'if-then' sentence. The thought represented in the antecedent of a conditional statement is unasserted: 'p' occurs unasserted in 'if p then q'. For example, if I think or say to myself, 'If a thunderstorm spoils our crops, we shall starve to death', the thought of a thunderstorm destroying our crops occurs unasserted. And it is no part of the concept of entertaining this thought that I imagine (seeing) our crops being destroyed by rain and lightning, even though I may be idiosyncratically inclined to do so. All that I have to do is entertain the *possibility* of the occurrence of the calamitous event, and this need not involve my forming any kind of mental picture of the event. In short, I do not have to imagine the actualization of the possible situation. I simply have to grasp, or bear in mind, that there is a climatic condition the obtaining of which will cause us to starve to death.

It seems to me that Johnson's entertainment of the thought about Desdemona's fate is comparable to one's entertaining the thought of the possibility of a thunderstorm spoiling his crops. Johnson is not imagining Desdemona being suffocated to death, but simply letting the thought enter his mind in the way of understanding that a woman can be such a victim of her husband's vindictive jealousy. For Johnson the thought of Desdemona's fate is, in essence, a disguised thought about the possibility of a woman's having that fate. His focal attention is directed towards the *depiction* of Desdemona's plight—which is essentially the depiction of an eventuality in the life of an unfortunate woman—rather than on the life depicted, which constitutes the intentional object of one's emotional appreciation of Desdemona. Thus his intentional attitude is not an attitude of imagination in the sense in which one uses this mental capacity to represent to oneself the fictional woman dying tragically in a fictional world.

In contrast, Robinson's way of entertaining the thought is to imagine what the thought refers to, or purports to refer to. It consists in his being in an intentional state whereby he is able to bring the depiction and the depicted to a unity. He sees the performance not just as the depiction of a possibility, but as an imaginative actualization of the possibility in the 'person' of Desdemona. In other words, his intentional attitude does not stop where Johnson's attitude stops, namely at the artistic representation or depiction itself, but extends to reach out to the 'intentional world' in which the depicted situation actualizes itself. By dint of the imagination, he perceives through the depiction or artistic representation the transfiguration of the tragic life of Desdemona.

I said earlier that it is not possible to give a non-circular explanation of fictional emotions by reference to an unqualified notion of empathy. But at this point I want to argue that invoking a qualified notion of empathy is very helpful to a solution of the problem. To show this it is necessary first to analyze the concept of empathy. Basically, the structure of empathy consists of two dimensions: affective and imaginative. The affective dimension represents a feeling or emotion which the empathizer experiences when he thinks about another person's thoughts and feelings. The imaginative dimension consists in his imaginatively representing the thoughts and feelings of the other person. When he feels with the other person, his feeling occurs in the very act of imagining the mental state of the other. In this sense we might say that empathy involves a confluence of feeling and imagination in a single mental state.

It would not be question-begging, I think, to use part of this notion to explain fictional emotion, namely empathy as containing only the imaginative dimension. In so far as this aspect of empathy is concerned, the empathizer imagines the other person's feelings by sincerely adopting that person's psychological point of view. It is from this point of view that he then looks at the world—the world as it appears to the person with whom he empathizes. Thus, in imagining the psychological perspective of the other person, the empathizer imagines himself as the subject inherent in that perspective.

This truncated version of empathy is also pertinent as an appropriate description of Robinson's mental attitude towards works of fiction. In watching the unfolding of Desdemona's fate, he envisages 'this' woman's life undergoing a certain course of action and events. His envisagement includes an 'inner' perception of her mental states, which implies that he sincerely adopts her psychological point of view—that viewpoint from which the world appears to her as horrendously inauspicious. It is Desdemona's own psychological perspective, inherent in her traumatic existential predicament, that predominantly determines the nature of his attention. And in imagining her as entangled in this predicament, he imagines himself as the subject of those feelings which occur to her in the midst of utter helplessness.

It may be wondered how the notion of empathy in its imaginative dimension is applicable to a case like the enraged lion case mentioned earlier. For in this case there is nothing analogous to empathy for another person or individual; there is nothing for the empathizer to identify with. How can a fictional fear of an enraged lion be explained by reference to the imaginative dimension of empathy? Whose psychological perspective does the subject imaginatively adopt here? The answer is that the subject, in this case, envisages himself being in a situation deemed to be threatening and dangerous. In imaginatively representing the movements of the lion in its enraged state, he also imagines himself situated helplessly against the lion. By leaving his own point of view as he actually is, he adopts an alien psychological perspective from which an endangered self looks at the world.

The idea of 'envisagement', used above, is of substantial importance to my argument, and hence I shall clarify it in relation to what might be termed 'mere thinking'—both being species of unasserted thoughts. Indeed, it is in terms of this distinction that I intend to spell out the crucial difference in the intentionality of Robinson's mental state from that of the art critic, Johnson. Basically the difference between envisagement and mere thinking is phenomenological. Envisagement is an act of imagination that is aptly accountable by reference to perceptual experience. The envisaged scene or situation is describable in those very terms that are employed in describing a perceptual experience of the scene or situation. Envisagement, as it were, mirrors perceptual experience.

On the other hand, merely thinking about a situation involves no more than just having the thought that the situation is thus and so. It is no more than what Frege calls 'the apprehension of a thought'. (Frege, 1956, p. 22ff.) What the stating of such a thought entails is an apprehension of the possibility of the situation. Also, merely thinking about a situation does not involve 'picturing' the situation to oneself (let alone picturing oneself in the situation). In contrast, envisagement is an experiential mode of thinking about something. Phenomenologically speaking, the envisaged situation stands to the imaginer in much the same way as the actual counterpart of it stands to the perceiver.[5]

Now I want to connect the claim that Robinson's emotional response to the depiction of Desdemona's fate involves the operation of empathetic imagination with the other claim that empathetic imagination (in its truncated version) occurs in the experiential mode of thinking which I have entitled 'envisagement'. The art critic, Johnson, who does not respond to Desdemona's fate with any emotion, is merely thinking about the depicted situation. His appreciation of what he watches does not take the form of envisagement; it is not founded on empathetic imagination. Hence the possibility of bringing to life the intentional world is not open to him. In short, the difference in our ways of watching and appreciating the fictional situation amounts to our entertaining the unasserted thought (about Desdemona's fate) from two different psychological vantage points: internally or from the inside, and externally or from the outside. Envisagement occurs from the internal point of vantage; mere thinking occurs from the external point of vantage.

One major question arises, however, concerning the dissimilarity in the modes of conceiving Desdemona's fate. Given the fact that both Johnson and Robinson appreciate the fictional situation under the guidance of the same regulative conception (i.e. the evaluative belief), how is it that their individual modes of entertaining the unasserted thought are so radically diverse? To answer this question, it is necessary to inquire into the nature and role of the evaluative belief in determining the diversity of one's attitudes to fiction.

It must be noted that the evaluative beliefs involved in emotional responses to various episodes and states of affairs are too complex to be described transparently. The complexity derives from the very

---

[5] In making the distinction between 'envisaging' something and 'merely thinking' about it I draw upon a similar distinction introduced by Richard Wollheim: namely between 'envisagement' and 'thoughts being thought'. The following passage is relevant to what I am developing here:

When I envisage a scene or situation, it is no longer simply that there is a thought before my mind—of which I may ask whether it occurs to me or whether I think it—there is now, let us say, a person or a group of persons before my mind. What is meant by this is that I am now able to say how the person looks, what he is doing or wearing here and now, what present feeling he arouses in me—not necessarily all these things, some of them—in a way which is not open to me if I am merely thinking of him. (Wollheim, 1973, p. 37)

nature of the contexts of life in which these emotions arise. Some vagueness seems to be built into the descriptive content of such beliefs. It is impossible, for instance, to state the evaluative belief about Desdemona's fate, held by Johnson and Robinson, in a single proposition, in the way the evaluative belief about enraged lions can be stated. The appreciation of the plight of Desdemona is grounded in a general conception of life and a conception of what it is for a life to end tragically, so that any emotional response to this plight is a response to a very complex object. Any plausible specification of the belief involved in that response, therefore, is most likely to include some subsidiary beliefs, or to refer to other beliefs conceptually implicated by the main belief. Whatever the case may be, the belief is going to be stated in terms of a set of propositions which will roughly—and perhaps sufficiently—represent what the belief is essentially about.

For the sake of explanatory convenience, let us assume that Johnson and Robinson hold the evaluative belief which consists of a set of propositions $p_1, p_2, p_3, \ldots p_n$, and call this set *EB*. What this is meant to encapsulate is the thought (very roughly): 'It is utterly tragic for an innocent woman to be suffocated to death by her husband, whose jealousy for her is created by another person's clandestine manipulation.' Concerning the question why both are not led by this belief to entertain the relevant unasserted thought from the same psychological perspective, I want to consider the possibility of different ways in which the same belief gets applied to the thought they both entertain.

It seems to me that there are basically two types of application of the evaluative belief to the unasserted thought. I shall describe them as 'straight' and 'crooked' applications. The belief has a straight application if no other beliefs, which do not have any conceptual connection with the main belief (i.e. which are not part of the set of propositions representing the main belief), or which are such that they contest, or throw suspicion on, the truth or plausibility of the belief, interferes with this belief when the person watches the fictional performance under its regulative influence. Alternatively, the belief has a crooked application if other beliefs, not strictly relevant to it, or not conceptually implicated by it, or beliefs which tend to raise doubt about the acceptability of the main belief, exert their diverse influences over it when the person is engaged in appreciating the performance or scene. Now these two features need spelling out.

For *EB* to be straightforwardly applied to Robinson's appreciation of the depiction of Desdemona's plight, it must be such that he sincerely takes *EB* to be true, in some sense, and hence does not doubt its authenticity.[6] Besides, there must not be any intervention of competing or conflicting beliefs and other cognitive considerations that might inhibit the *EB* from gaining ascendency. For example, thoughts such as 'this is a more sophisticated performance than the one I watched last month', or 'Desdemona's fate is not as tragic as the fate of Joan of Arc', must not enter his mind during his attention to the scene. In short, the *EB* must be insulated against all such extraneous forces that might weaken its strength or importance. For such forces will bring about a deflection in the direction of influence of the *EB*, thereby weakening, or even stopping, its causal contribution.

The *EB* has a crooked application when the above-mentioned factors permeate it, or deflect its direction of influence on to the unasserted thought. When it is surrounded by these other factors, the *EB* is denied its singular effect upon the act of entertaining the unasserted thought. This point might be clarified with the help of an example. When you are very sad at the death of a close relative or friend, your emotional state is explained in part by reference to the belief that someone of immense value to your life has been lost, and you will never be able to love and be loved by the deceased. But if you come to know that two of your friends or neighbours have also been in the same emotional state as yours due to similar reasons, your mental state is very likely to change into one of relatively moderate sadness; you may then no longer be in grief. Then you may go on to consider that thousands of others are going through a similar lot and millions of others are afflicted by much more serious problems of life.

These considerations, and the beliefs inherent in them, would then form a constellation within which your regulative belief would be submerged. Your belief would then be prevented from gaining the kind of ascendency which it enjoyed at first. It is not that your belief would be altered into a different belief by being enmeshed in the web of these other beliefs. Rather, this web of beliefs would

---

[6] The determination of truth or falsity of such evaluative beliefs has to take place within a value-theoretic scheme—a scheme that considers the subjectivity or objectivity of their status in relation to truth. Evaluative beliefs such as 'enraged lions are dangerous to humans', on the other hand, can more easily be accorded truth-values. For the fact that, given normal human conditions and responses, one finds the approach of an enraged lion threatening is good enough evidence for the truth of this evaluative statement.

exert a certain influence as a result of which your original belief would lose a great deal of its dynamism. Further, when global considerations prevail in your mind with greater force and persuasion, it is quite possible that your belief would sink into a kind of inertia. As a corollary to this, you might be able to attain equanimity and not feel any sadness at all. The deeply personal commitment embedded in the heart of your original belief would be extirpated, thus leaving you as a detached or impersonal spectator of the phenomenon.

Now I want to say that one can be such a detached or impartial audience with regard to a fictional performance as well. Johnson is such an audience. Though the fictional situation is watched and appreciated in accordance with an evaluative belief, this audience is not under the singular influence of this belief. The belief, in its crooked or deflected application, has only the intellectual, impersonal effect of allowing him merely to think of a woman's possible plight. There is an assembly of beliefs and other cognitive considerations interlocking with the *EB* in his mind. Hence the *EB* acts as a purely intellectual paradigm in terms of which he thinks about a possible situation in the life of an unfortunate woman when watching the performance.

But the *EB*, in its straight application in Robinson's case, has the singular effect of inspiring him to entertain the unasserted thought in the form of envisagement. This envisagement facilitates him to adopt, or identify with, the psychological point of vantage of Desdemona in her critical condition. So, in effect, the ability to imagine himself as the subject inherent in another psychological perspective is due to the unintervened influence of the *EB*. This is why his response to what he watches is emotional.

There is a further point that must be added to the above account. One reason why Johnson remains emotionally unaffected may also be that the character Desdemona is not the central figure of his attention. He may not only be thinking about Desdemona's fate, but may equally be thinking about Iago's dexterity in psychological manipulation, Othello's paranoid insecurity and Cassio's innocuous position in the total situation. In a sense his overall attitude has the character of being, so to speak, equidistributed between all the *dramatis personae*. In consequence, the possibility of there arising an overriding *EB*, able to exert its singular effect upon the thought of any particular fictional character, is nullified. There is no uniquely linear connection, in such a case, between an *EB* and an unasserted thought.

Contrasted with the above, Robinson's attention is focussed on a particular character, namely Desdemona. She constitutes the principal figure in his unasserted thought, while the others appear as peripheral figures alongside her. Correspondingly, there is an overriding *EB* with which the particular unasserted thought establishes a unique relationship. It is only when such a relationship between an overriding *EB* and a centrally focussed unasserted thought is solidified that an emotional response to a fictional character is made possible.

From our discussions in this section the point emerges that the right sort of combination of the evaluative belief and the unasserted thought provides both necessary and sufficient conditions of emotional responses to fiction. And it is only when the entertainment of the unasserted thought takes the form of envisagement, which is explicable by reference to the imaginative dimension of empathy, that the combination actually becomes a causally efficacious condition of emotional response.

5.4. CIRCUMSCRIBING THE INTENTIONAL HORIZON

Though I have laid down the conditions of the possibility of fictional emotions, I have not yet tried to characterize the nature of the intentional object of such an emotion. In other words, I have not addressed myself to the question of *what* we are emotional about when we feel fictional fear, pity, anger, or sadness. Since there is no existential belief in the constitution of fictional emotions, one may be said to feel fear for nothing, pity no one, be angry with nobody or sad about nothing. Evaluative beliefs, by themselves, only bring to mind kinds of objects, not particular objects. The imagination, on the other hand, produces mental constructs, not any mysterious entities. Is it then that fictional emotions are directed towards fictional mental constructs?

It has been suggested by Lamarque, as we saw in Chapter Two (Section 3), that we should distinguish between being emotional about the *thing* itself, and being emotional about the *thought* of the thing. Thus, to take fear as an example, while a real-life fear is directed towards the thing which is found frightening, a fictional fear is a case of being frightened by the *thought* of the thing. But I think that this suggestion does not help demarcate or characterize the object of fictional fear. For even in the case of real-life fear it is not the thing *per se* but the thing *as* I think of it, or *as* I hold beliefs about it, that frightens me. It is the thought or belief that the thing in question is dangerous or harmful or disagreeable which forms an essential constituent of fear.

It may be argued, however, that the distinction is helpful in that a fictional fear is a fear for the thought of a thing which does not exist, whereas a real-life fear is directed towards the thing which is believed to exist (and of course believed to be dangerous). As such, in the latter case the intentional arrow hits on an extensionally identifiable target that lies beyond the thought. But in the former case the intentional arrow hits only the thought, or does not go beyond the thought, such that the thought itself constitutes the object of fictional fear. The frightening quality associated with the thing is, as it were, attributed to the thought itself.

Lamarque's distinction, if and when interpreted in the above way, presumably is worth pursuing. However, Lamarque does want to mystify, in any way, thoughts as the objects of emotional attitudes. In order to prevent any such mystification, he argues that thoughts are identifiable in a *de dicto* fashion, such that the intentional arrow of fictional emotions actually hit certain propositions or descriptions. As he writes (to cite an earlier-quoted remark), 'when we respond emotionally to fictional characters we are responding to mental representations or thought-contents identifiable through descriptions derived in suitable ways from the propositional contents of fictional sentences'. (Lamarque, p. 302) He seems to allow no *de re* interpretation of the intentional object, as can be seen from the following remark (once quoted in Chapter Two): 'Stated baldly, when Desdemona enters our world she enters not as a person, not as an individual, not even as an imaginary being, but as a complex set of descriptions with their customary senses'. (p. 299)

Nevertheless, Lamarque does not seem to be free from vacillation with regard to the interpretation—*de re* or *de dicto*—of the intentional object. For he feels that, although he is quite inclined to favour a *de dicto* reading of fictional characters when analyzed from the semantic point of view, there is also another point of view no less important than the former. It is the viewpoint of assessing the quality and character of the psychological state involved in aesthetic experience which warrants a *de re* reading. We can witness Lamarque's divided mind when he qualifiedly says that

although it [his theory] incorporates a *de dicto* account of fictional characters, it acknowledges the pull of *de re* accounts; fictions comprise sets of ideas, many having correlates in reality, and these ideas invite an imaginative supplementation and exploration. In connection with fictional characters this 'filling in' process is not unlike that of *coming to know another human being*. (Lamarque, p. 302, italics original)

The italicized phrase quoted above is strongly indicative of Lamarque's partial but compelling desire to construe the intentional object in *de re* terms. It suggests that the intentional arrow of fictional emotions does not hit a mere propositional target erected out of the senses of fictional sentences. Rather, the intentionality of fictional emotions is more authentically describable in ways that are appropriate to describing the intentionality of real-life emotions.

Lamarque is not alone in wishing to recognize, albeit rather half-heartedly, the desirability of a *de re* reading of the fictional object. In a much more positive manner, Mounce advocates a *de re* construal of the intentional object of these emotions. With reference to our emotional response to Anna Karenina Mounce writes: 'Anna is more than an illustration of a point, as she is more than an element in a complex [language-]game, precisely in this: she is an object of our emotions'. (Mounce, p. 192)

It appears, however, that the problem does not admit of solution in any unequivocal terms. But I think that some light can be thrown on the problem by having recourse to a famous epistemological distinction put forward by Russell, namely that of 'knowledge by acquaintance' and 'knowledge by description'. (Russell, 1912, Ch. 5) From the objective, third-person point of view there can be no gainsaying that the object of a fictional emotion has to be construed in terms that are appropriate to delineating an object known by description only. The subject as it were gets hold of the object or character through a fictional description, or a fictional (that is aesthetic) medium. Therefore it seems necessary that the emotional state be characterized in *de dicto* terms as having a propositional object.

On the other hand, if we adopt the subjective, first-person point of view and analyse the situation, we seem to feel constrained to describe the mental state of the subject in terms that are appropriate to delineating an experience of someone claiming to know the fictional character by acquaintance. Our subject would describe his emotional state in much the same terms in which he would describe a real-life counterpart of that emotion. Any analysis of his inner state that reduces it to a mere propositional attitude will not fully capture the actual content and character of the state. There seems to be something more built into the phenomenological structure of fictional emotions than that which admits of being described as mere propositional attitudes. It might be said, metaphorically but not misleadingly, that the 'logical space' created by fictional sentences or descriptions, or by other aesthetic media, for the depiction of characters and events, is transformed by the imagination into an 'existential space'. And the existential vacuum, left by the absence of the existential belief, is 'filled in' by the imagination—not with any inscrutable imaginary objects or persons, but with experiential contents that demand a kind of *de re* construal of their intentionality.

From these considerations, I want to say that the question of *what* we are moved by when we respond to a fictional character or state of affairs admits of a twofold answer. And the two sides of the answer correspond to the two elements united to form the complex thought-process underlying a fictional emotion, namely the evaluative belief and the unasserted thought. Viewed from the standpoint of the unasserted thought in this thought-complex, the intentionality of fictional emotions can be accorded a *de dicto* reading. For in the absence of the existential belief, or in view of the fact that the object is fictional, the value of the variable 'Y' in sentence-forms of the kind 'X is (fictionally) emotional about Y' is always provided by a proposition or description that specifies the object of the emotion. One might say that the grammatical object-phrase of such a sentence is always an *un*disguised description.

On the other hand, what accounts for the plausibility of a *de re* construal of this intentionality is the role of the evaluative belief. For it is this belief which endows causal dynamism to the thought-complex on which a fictional emotion is founded, thereby making the subject experience the emotion in a way that requires the experience to be described in *de re* terms—that is, in terms of feeling an emotion towards some actual object, event or state of affairs. And it is by reference to the role of the evaluative belief that we can understand Lamarque's *de re* remark that an emotional appreciation of a fictional character is somewhat like '*coming to know another human being.*'

5.5. IMAGINATION AND DOXASTIC REPERTOIRE

If a *de re* reading of the intentionality of fictional emotions is accepted, then one must also concede that the structure of aesthetic experience—in so far as an aesthetic experience involves an emotional response to a depicted character or event—does not consist merely of a single stream of thought, namely unasserted thought. Rather, it consists of two intermingled streams—that of unasserted and asserted thoughts—such that the latter simultaneously flows as an undercurrent. It is in this regard that the Conservative theory differs from the Radical theory, which erroneously claims that the structure of aesthetic experience is wholly dictated by unasserted thought, namely imagination. My effort has been to show how evaluative beliefs of the appropriate kind invariably attach themselves to the contents of the imagination, thereby rendering the thought-complex partially asserted. Thus, it is the interplay between imagination and evaluative beliefs that constitutes the foundation of aesthetic or fictional emotions.

Now I want to relate the fact that the asserted component regulates and influences the unasserted component of the above-mentioned thought-complex within the structure of aesthetic experience, to a more comprehensive fact about how our general, value-laden conceptions about the world in relation to ourselves get integrated with our imaginative mode of thinking. Our response to the world and ourselves is, to a large extent, emotional. This response can be rephrased as the affective mode of apprehending the world and ourselves. We perceive objects and persons with fear, anger, hatred, love, horror, jealousy regret, resentment, indignation, gratitude and so on. From the time we learn to apprehend the world emotionally, we tend to form an enduring structure of various beliefs and conceptions upon which these emotional responses are founded—which we might describe as the *doxastic repertoire* at our disposal. The specific emotions that occur in us when we appreciate various situations of life in the light of the doxastic repertoire are spontaneous. It is this repertoire that comprises all our evaluative paradigms, in terms of which reality is affectively apprehended by us. Given our natural inclinations and human nature in general, the specific beliefs contained in the repertoire force us to feel in definite ways towards appropriate objects.

There are other times, however, during which we do not actually encounter the objects of our emotions, but encounter them in the imagination—either in the form of willed imaginative representation of the objects, or in perceiving fictional depictions of them. Since the objects are fictional, we do not feel 'committed' towards them in the way we commit ourselves to actual objects of emotional encounter. Nevertheless, the doxastic repertoire is not forgotten, or set aside, when we envisage ourselves being in these fictional situations. Rather, the repertoire remains with us in unaltered form. And since it remains with us, we carry an 'image' of the emotional reality defined in accordance with the repertoire. Correspondingly, we also carry with us a sense of *ideal* commitment towards the imagined spectacle. And it is by virtue of this repertoire that a fictional episode is placed in its proper context and appreciated. As such, the constituent beliefs or conceptions of the repertoire retain enough causal potency to be actualized even in imagined contexts. Thus our being moved by depicted fictional scenarios is explained by the fact that causally efficacious beliefs and conceptions govern our imaginative attention towards these scenarios.

In the light of the above, we can now understand better the point—rightly underscored by Scruton—about the essential continuity between fictional or aesthetic emotions and real-life emotions. Our emotional response to fiction is a reflection of our normal emotional response to incidents of real life. Fictional emotions are rooted in the normal emotional reality of our daily life. They are the extended, and sometimes perhaps sophisticated, expressions of the very attitudes to life and the world which underlie the occurrence of real-life emotions. What accounts for this common root, and the essential continuity of the former with the latter, is the enduring doxastic repertoire, which is carried along by us as we enter into a fictional world. We remain bound to the repertoire even when we leave the real world in order to appreciate the lives of fictional characters and the twists and turns of fictional events. This conceptual bond in turn explains our ultimate anchorage in reality. If we understand these linkages, it becomes evident to us what bridges the intangible gulf between fiction and reality.

CONCLUSION

In this book I have examined the problem of emotional response to fiction by concentrating on the allegation that such responses involve us in incoherence and inconsistency. We normally do not believe that fictional characters exist or that fictional events occur. Yet we respond to them with various emotions that, it seems, can rationally be accounted for only by imputing to us appropriate beliefs about the fate of the characters or the twists and turns of the events. Since this seeming paradox is about belief, I found it right to start with an analysis of the relation between emotion and belief. I argued that appropriate beliefs are essential to the constitution of emotions *proper*. The intentionality of these emotions is secured by the beliefs that are suitably included in them. Emotions may thus be characterized as belief-dependent mental states.

I then argued for the view that the appropriate beliefs are linked with the relevant emotions in a non-contingent causal nexus. Beliefs are causally efficacious in generating emotions, even though emotions are identified and classified by reference to beliefs.

Given the causal-cum-conceptual role of belief in emotion, one has to make a special effort to explain the occurrence of emotions towards fiction. It is not just obvious that one can identify an appropriate belief that would play the causal-cum-conceptual role in a fictional emotion. Indeed, it has been held that, if we do not believe that the character exists or the event occurs, we cannot form an appropriate belief about the character or event and *a fortiori* we shall not emotionally respond to the object in question. Yet we *do* respond to fictions in ways that are characteristically similar to those of responding to analogous real-life people and events.

It is in the context of this discrepancy between fact and principle that I discussed Radford's thesis of the irrationality of fictional emotions. I argued that Radford's view is fundamentally wrong, since it denies fictional emotions even the minimally rational structure of an emotion. To concede that fictional emotions are inescapably paradoxical, in that they occur without satisfying the necessary condition for the occurrence of an emotion, is to forfeit the right to categorize these mental states as *emotions*.

By way of trying to establish the rationality of fictional emotions I critically reviewed two prominent theories, namely the Reformist and the Radical theories, which attempt to show the coherence of these emotions in two different ways. The Reformist theory aims at resolving the alleged paradox by arguing that it is make-beliefs or second-order beliefs that play a causal-cum-conceptual role in fictional emotions. The Radical theory argues that this key role is played by the imagination, which is a species of unasserted thought and is essentially contrasted with belief. I criticized both theories on the ground that neither make-belief nor second-order belief nor the imagination can constitute a causal condition for eliciting emotions. None of these mental states or attitudes can be a causally potent substitute for belief proper. Hence I argued that these theories fail to account for our response to fiction and thus do not offer a genuine rebuttal of Radford's allegation.

On the basis of the above observations, I proposed the Conservative theory, intending to give my own account of fictional emotions. My purpose was twofold. On the one hand, I proceeded in conformity with the *spirit* of the Reformist theory and tried to identify a genuine belief that plays its legitimate causal-cum-conceptual role in the evocation of our response to fiction—namely an evaluative belief. When we appreciate a certain fictional character or event and feel a particular emotion towards the character or event, our emotional appreciation is made possible partly by the fact that we form an appropriate belief about the fate of the character or the nature of the event. And this evaluative belief is the same as the corresponding evaluative belief that we form about an analogous real life character or event when we respond to the person or situation with a specific emotion. I argued that it is this similarity of evaluative beliefs involved both in fictional and real-life emotions that explains the 'necessary continuity'—rightly emphasized by the Radical theory—between the two emotions.

On the other hand, I found it necessary to follow the *direction* of the Radical theory and endorsed, with qualification, the view that fictional emotions are partly founded on imagination. The qualification is that, as a species of unasserted thought, the imagination is essentially contrasted with existential belief, not with evaluative belief. Whereas the object of a real-life emotion is the object of an existential belief, the object of a fictional emotion is an object of the imagination. Thus the imagination plays an alternative conceptual role in place of the existential belief and transforms our psychological perspective in order to enable us to adopt the standpoint of an 'insider' of a fictional world.

The conclusion of my argument is that it is the interaction between an evaluative belief and the imagination that suffices to generate an emotional response to a fictional character or event. The alleged paradox disappears when it is realized that we can form an evaluative belief about a character or event without at the same time having an existential belief about the character or event. A fictional depiction of a life or situation is as much the object of some evaluative belief as a description of an analogous actual life or situation: the same evaluative paradigm is applicable to both cases. As a genuine, first-order belief, the evaluative belief is a causally potent factor in the evocation of an emotion. Whereas in the real-life case this potency is actualized when the evaluative belief is combined with the existential belief, in the fictional case this potency is actualized when the evaluative belief is appropriately united with the imagination.

I acknowledge that the solution provided in my theory builds on the two theories which I discussed and criticized in the thesis and that it does not entirely supplant either theory. I agree with the Reformist theorists that it is necessary to identify the role of a belief in order to account for the rationality of fictional emotions, but disagree with their contention that a make-belief or a second-order belief can provide a causal-cum-rational explanation of these emotions. I agree with the Radical theorist that our emotional response to fiction is founded on imagination, but dissent from his view that belief has no role to play in eliciting such responses. Thus I try to bring the two theories under a kind of methodological synthesis, whereby I create a new theory that provides both necessary and sufficient conditions for the occurrence of a fictional emotion.

It may be wondered what implication my theory has for the importance of fictional emotions and whether this theory sheds any illumination for a general account of the nature and significance of fiction. The central question is why we are willing to grant the 'reality' of fictions and not dismiss them as 'mere fictions': that is to say, why we value fictions as a lofty human enterprise. I think that my theory provides an answer to this question at least from one important point of view. By identifying the essential role of an evaluative belief in the appreciation of fictions, it demonstrates that we endow fictions with reality by virtue of an imaginative extension of paradigmatic evaluative conceptions to cover fictional cases. We bring fictional characters and events under the scope of genuine evaluative beliefs, much as we bring other human beings and their situations under an evaluative paradigm that grows out of an empathetic understanding (*verstehen*) of their condition. Our ability to appreciate fictional characters is of a piece with our capacity to appreciate people who are caught up in circumstances of which we are also possible victims. Thus the mode of response made by us towards an episode of a work of fiction can be regarded as an extension of the mode of response made by an onlooker towards a similar actual event.

To appreciate fictions is, to some extent, also to fictionalize ourselves, so that we may involve ourselves in a kind of metaphoric participation with fictional characters in some fictional world. Fiction then becomes a metaphor for life and our life is transfigured into the character in whose life we participate. But, as Arthur Danto points out, though the structure of artistic metaphoric transfigurations is like the structures of making-believe or pretending to be what one actually is not, it is also significantly different. Whereas pretending always involves knowing that one is not what one is pretending to be, and always ceases, like a game, when it is done, artistic transfiguration embodies an element of truth in that it involves an identification of oneself with the transfigured life. As Danto writes: 'artistic metaphors are different to the extent that they are in some way true: to see oneself as Anna [Karenina] is in some way to *be* Anna [Karenina], and to see one's life as *her* life, so as to be changed by experience of being her'. (Danto, 1981, p. 173) He then generalizes this point in the following passage:

Art, if a metaphor at times on life, entails that the not unfamiliar experience of being taken out of oneself by art—the familiar artistic illusion—is virtually the enactment of a metaphoric transformation with oneself as subject: you are what the work ultimately is about, a commonplace person transfigured into an amazing woman. (p. 173)

Danto's claim that artistic metaphors are in some sense true can, I believe, be squared with my argument that we bring fictional characters under the scope of true evaluative beliefs and appreciate them in a mode of response which is an extension of the mode of our response to actual people. And combined with the plasticity of the imagination, true evaluative beliefs can indeed bring about 'metaphoric transformation' of ourselves, thereby enabling us genuinely to respond to fictional beings.

BIBLIOGRAPHY

Alston, William P. (1967), 'Emotion and Feeling', in Edwards, Paul
(ed.), *The Encyclopedia of Philosophy*, vol. 2 (New York and
London: Macmillam & The Free Press), pp. 479–86.
Aristotle (1941), *De Anima*, translated by Smith, J. A. in McKeon
(ed.) (1941), pp. 535–606.
———— (1967), *Poetics*, translated by Else, Gerald F. (Ann Arbor:
The University of Michigan Press).
Aune, Bruce (1967), *Knowledge, Mind and Nature* (New York:
Random House).
Bedford, Errol (1956–7), 'Emotions', *Proceedings of the Aristotelian
Society*, LVII, pp. 281–304.
Casey, John (ed.) (1971), *Morality and Moral Reasoning* (London:
Methuen & Co.).
Danto, Arthur (1981), *The Transfiguration of the Commonplace*
(Cambridge, Massachusetts: Harvard University Press).
Davidson, Donald (1963), 'Actions, Reasons and Causes', *Journal
of Philosophy*, vol. LX, pp. 685–99.
———— (1969), 'On Saying That', in Davidson & Hintikka (1969),
pp. 158–174.
———— (1982), 'Paradoxes of Irrationality', in Wollheim & Hopkins
(1982), pp. 289–305.
Davidson, Donald & Hintikka, Jakko (eds.) (1969), *Words and
Objections* (Dordrecht: D. Reidel).
Davies, Stephen (1983), 'The Rationality of Aesthetic Responses',
British Journal of Aesthetics, vol. XXIII, pp. 38–47.
De Sousa, Ronald (1979) 'The Rationality of Emotions', *Dialogue*,
vol. XVIII, pp. 41–63; reprinted in Rorty (1980), pp. 127–51.
Dummett, Michael (1973), *Frege: Philosophy of Language* (London:
Duckworth).
Frege, Gottlob (1952), 'Sense and Reference', in Geach & Black
(1952).
———— (1956), 'The Thought: A Logical Inquiry', *Mind*, vol. LXV,
pp. 289–311; reprinted in Strawson (ed.), (1967), pp. 17–38.
Geach, Peter (1957), *Mental Acts* (London: Routledge & Kegan
Paul).
Geach, Peter & Black, Max (eds.) (1952), *The Philosophical Writings*

of Gottlob Frege (Oxford: Basil Blackwell).

Gordon, R. (1974), 'The Aboutness of Emotions', *American Philosophical Quarterly*, vol. II, pp. 27–36.

Green, O. H. (1972), 'Emotion and Belief', in Rescher, Nicholas (ed.) (1972), pp. 24–40.

Guthrie, J. L. (1981), 'Self-Deception and Emotional Response to Fiction', *British Journal of Aesthetics*, vol. XXI, pp. 65–75.

Hampshire, Stuart (ed.) (1966), *Philosophy of Mind* (New York & London: Harper and Row).

Hanlfing, Oswald (1983), 'Real Life, Art and the Grammar of Feeling',*Philosophy*, vol. LVIII, pp. 237–43.

Honderich, Ted & Burnyeat, Myles (ed.) (1979), *Philosophy As It Is* (Harmondsworth: Penguin Books Ltd.).

Johnson, Samuel (1765), *Preface to the Plays of William Shakespeare*, in Vickers (ed.) (1979), pp. 55–176.

Kenny, Anthony (1963), *Action, Emotion and Will* (London: Routledge & Kegan Paul.

Kenrick, William (1765), 'Johnson Attacked', in Vickers (ed.) (1979), pp. 182–210.

Lamarque, Peter (1981), 'How can we Fear and Pity Fictions?', *British Journal of Aesthetics*, vol. XXI, pp. 291–304.

Lazarus, Richard 1982), 'Thoughts on the Relation between Emotion and Cognition', *American Psychologist*, vol. XXXVII, pp. 1019–24.

Lyons, William (1980), *Emotion* (Cambridge: Cambridge University Press).

McKeon, Richard (ed.) (1941), *The Basic Works of Aristotle* (New York: Random House).

Mounce, H. O. (1980), 'Art and Real Life', *Philosophy*, vol. LV, pp. 183–92.

Neu, Jerome (1977), *Emotion, Thought and Therapy* (London: Routledge & Kegan Paul; Berkeley: University of California Press).

—— (1980), 'Jealous Thoughts', in Rorty (ed.) 1980), pp. 425–64.

Novitz, David (1980), 'Fiction, Imagination and Emotion', *Journal of Aesthetics and Art Criticism*, vol. XXXVIII, pp. 279–88.

Pears, David (1982a), 'Motivated Irrationality', *Proceedings of the Aristotelian Society*, supplementary volume, vol. LVI, pp. 157–78.

—— (1982b) 'Motivated Irrationality, Freudian Theory and Cognitive Dissonance', in Wollheim & Hopkins (ed.) (1982), pp. 264–88.

Price, H. H. (1964), 'Half-Belief', *Proceedings of the Aristotelian Society*, supplementary volume, vol. XXXVIII, pp. 148–62.

Prichard, H. A. (1950), *Knowledge and Perception* (Oxford: Clarendon Press).

Radford, Colin (1975), 'How can we be moved by the fate of Anna Karenina?', *Proceedings of the Aristotelian Society*, supplementary volume, vol. LXIX, pp. 67–80.

—— (1977), 'Tears and Fiction', *Philosophy*, vol. LII, pp. 208–13.

—— (1982a), 'Philosophers and their Monstrous Thoughts', *British Journal of Aesthetics*, vol. XXII, pp. 61–3.

—— (1982b), 'Stuffed Tigers: A Reply to H. O. Mounce', *Philosophy*, vol. XVII, pp. 529–32.

Rescher, Nicholas (ed.) (1972), *Studies in the Philosophy of Mind*, Monograph Series, No. 6 of *American Philosophical Quarterly*.

Rorty, Amelie (ed.) (1980), *Explaining Emotions* (Berkeley, Los Angeles, London: University of California Press).

—— (1983), 'Fearing Death', *Philosophy*, vol. LVIII, pp. 175–88.

Russell, Bertrand (1912), *The Problems of Philosophy* (Oxford: Oxford University Press).

Ryle, Gilbert (1949), *The Concept of Mind* (London: MacMillan Press).

Sartre, J. P. (1962), *Sketch for a Theory of the Emotions*, translated by Mariet, Philip (London: Methuen & Co.).

Schaper, Eva (1978), 'Fiction and the Suspension of Disbelief', *British Journal of Aesthetics*, vol. XVIII, pp. 31–44.

Scruton, Roger (1971), 'Attitude, Belief and Reason', in Casey (ed.) (1971), pp. 25–100.

—— (1970–1), 'Intensional and Intentional Objects', *Proceedings of the Aristotelian Society*, vol. LXXI, pp. 187–208.

—— (1974), *Art and Imagination* (London: Methuen & Co.).

Searle, John (1979), *Expression and Meaning* (Cambridge: Cambridge University Press).

—— (1983), *Intentionality: An Essay in the Philosophy of Mind* (Cambridge: Cambridge University Press).

Shaffer, Jerome (1983), 'An Assessment of Emotions', *American Philosophical Quarterly*, vol. XX, pp. 161–73.

Skulsky, Harold (1980), 'On Being Moved by Fiction', *Journal of Aesthetics and Art Criticism*, vol. XXXI, pp. 5–14.

Solomon, Robert (1977), *The Passions: The Myth and Nature of Human Emotions* (New York, Garden City: Anchor Press/Doubleday).

Strawson, P. F. (ed.) (1967), *Philosophical Logic* (Oxford: Oxford University Press).
———— (1974), 'Imagination and Perception', in Strawson (1974), pp. 45–65.
———— (1974), *Freedom and Resentment and Other Essays*, (London: Methuen & Co.).
Taylor, Gabriele (1975), 'Justifying the Emotions', *Mind*, vol. LXXXIV, pp. 390–402.
———— (1975–6), 'Love', *Proceedings of the Aristotelian Society*, vol. LXXVI, pp. 147–64; reprinted in Honderich & Burnyeat (eds.) (1979), pp. 165–182.
Thalberg, Irving (1964), 'Emotion and Thought', *American Philosophical Quarterly*, vol. I, pp. 45–55, reprinted in Hampshire (ed.) (1966), pp. 201–25.
Urmson, J. O. (1976), 'Fiction', *American Philosophical Quarterly*, vol. XIII, pp. 153–7.
Vendler, Zeno (1972), *Res Cogitans: An Essay in Rational Psychology* (London & Ithaca: Cornell University Press).
Vickers, Brian (ed.) 1979), *Shakespeare: The Critical Heritage*, volume 5, 1765–1774 (London: Routledge & Kegan Paul).
Walton, Kendall (1978a), 'Fearing Fictions', *Journal of Philosophy*, vol. LXXV, pp. 5–27.
———— (1978b), 'How Remote are Fictional Worlds from the Real World?', *Journal of Aesthetics and Art Criticism*, vol. XXXVII, pp. 11–23.
Weston, Michael (1975), 'How can we be moved by the fate of Anna Karenina?', *Proceedings of the Aristotelian Society*, supplementary volume, LXIX, pp. 81–93.
Wilson, J. R. S (1972), *Emotion and Object* (Cambridge: Cambridge University Press).
Wittgenstein, Ludwig (1953), *Philosophical Investigations*, translated by Elizabeth Anscombe (Oxford: Basil Blackwell).
Wollheim, Richard (1967–8), 'Thought and Passion', *Proceedings of the Aristotelian Society*, vol. LXVIII, pp. 1–24.
———— (1973), 'The Mind and the Mind's Image of Itself', in Wollheim (1973), pp. 31–53.
———— (1973), *On Art and the Mind* (London: Allen Lane).
Wollheim, Richard and Hopkins, James (1982), *Philosophical Essays on Freud* (Cambridge: Cambridge University Press).
Wolterstorff, Nicholas (1980), *Works and Worlds of Art* (Oxford: Clarendon Press).

INDEX

Action
  intentionality of, see under
    Intentionality
  emotion without, 104–7
Aesthetic attitude, 60–3, 95
Aesthetic detachment, 108
Aesthetic emotion, 76–7, 81–95,
  101, 121
Aesthetic experience, 61n, 76–7, 89,
  120–1
Aesthetic response, 76, 82–5
Akrasia, 49–50
Alston, W. P., 10n, 127
Aristotle, 1, 33, 90n, 103, 127
Artistic illusion, 126
Assertion
  and language, 77–9
  and meaning, 78–9
  and thought, 3, 6–9, 31, 78–9, 92,
    102, 121
  and truth, 8–9
Aune, B., 78, 127

Beauty and truth, 8n
Bedford, E., 10n, 63n, 127
Belief
  and desire, 84–9, 105–7
  and emotion, 1–5, 9–31, 35–8, 44,
    46–8, 51–64, 70, 75–6, 83–5,
    93–5, 97–8, 116–17, 122–5 and
    passim
  and imagination, 3–4, 76–81, 90–5,
    98–100, 121–2, 124–6
  and knowledge, 52–3
  causal efficacy of, 3–4, 17, 22–6,
    63–4, 70, 90–5, 102–4, 115–17,
    123–5
  counterfactual, 62–3
  evaluative and existential, 2, 4,
    12, 17–21, 24–6, 97–109, 113–17,
    121, 124–6
  first-order, 3, 50, 56–65, 69–71, 75

  second-order, 3–4, 56–65, 67,
    74–6, 124–5
  thought and, 9–10, 26, 31, 42–3,
    48, 77–81
Blake, William, 8n
Brentano, F., 5
Burnyeat, M., 128

Casey, J., 127
Causation
  of emotion, 2–4, 22–7, 61–74,
    93–4, 123 and *passim*
  of fictional emotion, 3–4, 50–1,
    61–4, 67–8, 70–1, 74, 102–5 and
    passim
Conception of life, 40–1, 43, 114

Danto, A., 126–7
Davidson, D., 22–3 34–5, 36n, 78n,
  127
De dicto/de re interpretation (of
  intentionality), see under
  Intentionality
Depiction and the depicted, 110–11
De Sousa, R., 34, 127
Doxastic repertoire, 120–2
Dummett, M., 9, 79n, 127

Emotion
  and action, 88–9, 104–5, 105n
  as personal ideology, 105n
  inordinate, 36n
  make-believe, 68, 71, 73
  quasi-, 65–8, 67, 70–2, 84
  real-life, 2–3, 32, 49, 76–7, 81–2,
    84, 90–1, 97–8, 100, 102, 104–6,
    117–19, 122–4 and *passim*
  self-deceptive, 13
  without action, 104–7
Emotional reality, 4, 122
Empathetic attitude, 108
Empathetic imagination, 113

Belief cannot be the primitive
mode of intentionality. (pp 8-9)
Because intentionality can occur
without the commitment/judgement
element which belief involves.

⟶ Now (cf Commons) the way
 is open for the view that the
 primitive element in representation
 is not propositional at all.

"[In entertaining the thought of X as
 Y] the thought of Y is unpredicative
 attached to the thought of X — which is
 why it is impossible to formulate the
 thought in a that-clause." (p.9)

pp 14-18 — 'Formal object' of
          emotions & evaluative belief
          & evaluative properties.

P.23 "Basically an emotion consists of two
     units: first, a cognitive-evaluative
     aspect, which is the aspect of belief;
     second, an affective aspect consisting of
     certain sensational & psysiological states